THE HARDEST PARTS

techniques for effective non-fiction

Thomas Fensch

LMB

Lander Moore Books
Austin, Texas

Copyright © 1984 by Thomas Charles Fensch

All rights reserved. No part of this work may be reproduced or transmitted in any form by any means, electronic or mechanical, including photocopying and recording, or by any information storage or retrieval system, without permission in writing from Lander Moore Books, 13006 Sherbourne, Austin, Texas, 78729.

Printed in the United States of America.

9 8 7 6 5 4 3 2 1

The author has attempted wherever possible to use non-sexist language. No emphasis on the masculine is intended.

Library of Congress Card Number: 84-81603

ISBN 0-930751-01-9

ACKNOWLEDGMENTS

Grateful acknowledgment is made to the following for permission to print or reprint copyrighted material:

"The Three R's for Revitalizing Article Sales," which was first published in *Writer's Digest* is reprinted with permission of Larry Holden.

Material from Annette McGivney reprinted with permission of the author.

Material by Julie Albert printed with permission of the author.

"You, Me and Handguns," by Tom Wicker © 1980 by *The New York Times Company*, reprinted with permission.

Material from "Starting young is a key to working with Stutterers," by Michael Kernan, *Smithsonian* magazine, May, 1981, reprinted with permission of Michael Kernan, *Smithsonian* magazine.

Selections from "The Silent Season of a Hero" by Gay Talese reprinted with permission of Gay Talese.

Material by Gale Wiley printed with permission of the author.

Material from *The World of Oz* by Osborn Elliott, copyright © 1980 by Osborn Elliott.reprinted by permission of Viking Penguin, Inc.

The following excerpt is reprinted courtesy of *SPORTS ILLUSTRATED* from May 3, 1965, issue. Copyright © 1965, Time, Inc. "The Strange Fish and Stranger Times of Dr. Herbert R. Axelrod" by Robert H. Boyle.

The following excerpt is reprinted courtesy of *SPORTS ILLUSTRATED* from the Dec. 22-29, issue. Copyright © 1968, Time, Inc. "Where Nothing But Good Happens" by T.H. Kelly.

The following excerpt is reprinted courtesy of *SPORTS ILLUSTRATED* from Dec. 8, 1980, issue. Copyright ©1980, Time, Inc. "L.A.'s Fight Song: We Are Not Fam-i-lee" By Barry McDermott.

The following excerpt is reprinted courtesy of *SPORTS ILLUSTRATED* from the Nov. 3, 1980, issue. Copyright ©1980, Time, Inc. "Hey, Mister Fantasy Man" by Bob Ottum.

Excerpts from "On Being a Patient," which first appeared in the *Atlantic Monthly*, reprinted with permission of Stephen Becker.

Excerpts from MAGAZINE ARTICLE WRITING: SUBSTANCE AND STYLE by Betsy P. Graham. Copyright © 1980 by Holt, Rinehart and Winston. Reprinted by permission of Holt, Rinehart and Winston, CBS College Publishing.   Excerpts from "Ode to the Age of the Beetle," which first appeared in *Yankee* reprinted with permission of Robert J. Connors.

Sections from "Turn Your Home into a Solar Collector" by John. H. Ingersoll reprinted by permission from *Good Ideas*. Copyright © 1980 Armstrong World Industries, Inc.

Material from *Magazine Writer's Workbook* reprinted with permission of John C. Behrens, author of *Magazine Writer's Workbook* with Alex Haley.

Material from "Dumbarton Oaks; stately link from past to the present" by Michael Olmert, which was first published in *Smithsonian* magazine, May, 1981, reprinted with permission of Michael Olmert.

Excerpts from ON REPORTING THE NEWS reprinted by permission of New York University Press from ON REPORTING THE NEWS by William E. Burrows. Copyright © 1977 by New York University.

Material by Kelle Banks printed by permission of the author.

List of 10 topics under "Quotation Marks" found in the UPI Newswire Stylebook, pages 148-149, 1977 edition reprinted by permission of United Press International.

One paragraph from *The Changing Magazine* quoted, by permission, from *The Changing Magazine* by Ronald E. Wolseley. New York: Hastings House, 1973, p.8.

Material from *Freelance and Staff Writer* by William L. Rivers reprinted with permission of William L. Rivers.

Materials by David Lampe and Hal Higdon reprinted with permission.

Material from the *Popular Science Contributor's Guidelines* reprinted courtesy of *Popular Science* magazine.

"Sentinel at Niagara Falls" was first published in *Cavalier* magazine.

"Twelve Ways to End Your Article Gracefully" is reprinted courtesy of Robert L. Baker.

The author is grateful to the following members of the American Society of Journalists and Authors for their suggests and material: David Lampe; Hal Higdon; John H. Ingersoll; Dr. Dian Dincin Buchman; and Maurice Zolotov.

The author is also grateful to Gale Wiley; Jack Pickering; my father, Dr. Edwin A. Fensch; and my wife, Jean, for their thoughtful advice and support.

For Beatrice Driscoll—
with love and gratitude.

Other communications books
by Thomas Fensch:

film-making:
Films on the Campus (1970)

public communication:
Smokeys, Truckers, CB Radios & You (1976)

publishing:
Steinbeck and Covici:
The Story of a Friendship (1979)

CONTENTS

	Page
Introduction: Small-time thinking and Big-time thinking; Sober self-assessment and mad self-challenge	i
1. The contemporary American magazine and the free-lance writer	1
2. The article, part-by-part	5
3. *Curiosity, compulsive reading, contacts, commitment, expertise* ... where article ideas come from	17
4. *The progression of an article:* Externally, planning the article; Internally, structuring the article	21
5. *Braving the library* ... Researching the article and writing the outline	27
6. 25 tips—and then some—for better interviewing	33
7. *But what did it look like?* The art of observation ... *But I want to know why* ... The psychology of personality	43
8. *The top of page one* ... Types of leads: *the summary lead; the descriptive lead; the mosaic lead; the narrative lead; the anecdotal lead; the problem (or paradox) lead; the first-person (I) lead; the second-person (You) lead; the interior monologue lead; the flat statement lead; the parody lead; the simile or metaphor lead; the parody lead; the "false" lead; the What-Where-When (newspaper) lead; the Name-Prominent lead; the Diary-Timeline lead*	50
9. *The top of page one* ... Types of leads, Part Two: *the quotation lead; the question lead; the dual narrative lead; the unorthodox lead; the classified ad lead; the future-tense fictional lead; the shotgun lead; the historical updating lead; the historical perspective lead; the psychological lead*	67
10. Do's and Don't's of Writing Query Letters	79
11. Do's and Don't's of Mailing Manuscripts	90

12. A few words about style . . .
and non-sexist language; use of quotations and quotation marks; statistics; transitions; the deliberate and accidental double entendre; copyediting; pros and cons of the literary agent; the physical manuscript; theft of ideas and titles 92

13. Twelve Ways to End Your Article Gracefully 107

14. The Three R's for Revitalizing Article Sales 116

15. *Like a stranger in a strange land . . .*
Selling the regional article to the national magazine 123

16. Multiple sales: you can sell any article more than once
Any article 130

17. Writing the science article 143

18. Feature Techniques for television and radio reporters 150

Bibliography 159
Glossary 164
Index 172
About the Author 178

Introduction

Small-time thinking and *Big-time thinking; sober self-assessment* and *mad self-challenge.*

In article writing, as well as in all kinds of creative endeavor, there is a "big time" and there is a "small time." Small-time markets, because they are less competitive and more particularized and therefore less risky, have advantages for the beginner and for the part-time writer. But a small-time writer may occasionally want to try the big-time magazine or book publisher, either to find out if he or she belongs in the big time or just for the occasional satisfaction of "making it big."

For the professional writer who regularly hits the major markets and who makes a comfortable living at freelancing, the ideal is to "go over the top" from magazine articles to non-fiction books and from smaller sales to the best-seller lists. There are books which are critically reviewed but have modest sales, and then there are "blockbusters" which hit the top-selling charts and stay there, making the authors not only a comfortable royalty, but perhaps offering them a chance to write only a few select books.

In short, everyone's life is in part a sort of calculus of sober self-assessment within the marketplace of literature and commerce; everyone's life fluctuates between this sober self-assessment and mad self-challenge.

This book hopes to bridge the gap between the *small-time* and *big-time* markets; between *small-time* and *big-time* thinking. The *techniques* and *skills* suggested in this book have resulted in sales to small, special-interest magazines, as well as general, nationally-circulated magazines, by students at Ohio State University and the University of Texas and by writers elsewhere.

The reader should realize more than anything else that the writer sells not just expertise, grammar, spelling and punctuation, but *time*. One of the crucial differences between the small-time or part-time writer and the professional who makes a living at article writing is the fact that the professional knows *how much time each article is worth.* In the business world, the equivalent might be the term *cost-efficient*. Business leaders analyze whether a certain campaign is cost-efficient in terms of response; writers must learn that their *time* is extremely valuable. Professionals may turn down assignments when they discover that the research, writing and re-writing demand more time than the actual payment for the article. One magazine writer may set a minimum of $500 for each major-length article assignment; another $750, another $1,000 for a major piece. Less than their minimum results in too much work for too little payment to justify the time spent on each project.

Another key idea which professionals instinctively understand is: *begin as high as possible,* in the most prestigous, highest-paying markets. Some writers never get above the local or special-interest magazine because they don't aim for the highest markets. You'll never get there if you don't aim there. This book offers *technique* and *skills* which will enable the would-be writer to reach not only for the regional or special-interest market, but for the major, national magazines as well.

Why another book on article writing techniques? Times change. Previously, in the heyday of the "barber shop" men's magazines, as they were called, *True* and *Argosy* and *Saga,* the average length of a major feature piece was 4,000 to 5,000 words. Now the average is 2,500 words and still going down. With an article length of 5,000 words, the writer could afford to devote not just paragraphs but several manuscript pages to the lead; now, as the article length of many features is shrinking, the lead and all component parts of the article must be shorter. The writer must now capture the reader with a crisper lead and a shorter article.

The New Journalism of the 1960s and 1970s has also changed the magazine world. Tom Wolfe, Gay Talese, Truman Capote, Hunter S. Thompson, Norman Mailer and Joan Didion have all exerted a vast influence on readers as well as other writers. Now many major newspapers are using a magazine format; although this book emphasizes magazine treatment, this book is just as appropriate for newspaper feature writers as well.

Not only has time changed the article, but technology changes. In the heyday of *True* and *Argosy,* compact tape recorders were a novelty and word processors were unheard of. Now the hand-held tape recorder is a necessity and the word processor is becoming more and more important in the lives of authors and freelancers. Many magazines are now edited on video display terminals and large journalism schools teach VDT usage to undergraduate students, unheard of a few years ago.

The television "news magazine," such as *60 Minutes* and *20/20,* have borrowed the magazine format; thus it is important that this book contains Gale Wiley's chapter of feature writing techniques as they apply to the broadcast industry ("Feature Techniques for Television and Radio Reporters").

Small-time thinking to big-time thinking. Small-time markets to big-time markets. Contemporary techniques and skills. Sober self-assessment and mad self-challenge. That's what this book is all about.

Thomas Fensch

THE HARDEST PARTS

Chapter One

The Contemporary American Magazine and the Freelance Writer

There is no better time than now for an aspiring writer to begin writing and selling nonfiction articles: there are more magazines than ever and if the rates don't keep up with inflation (what does?), you can find a niche writing and selling to a vast variety of general and special-interest magazines.

The world of American magazines has always been a fascinating, dynamic world, populated with the greatest success stories and epic failures, fortunes won, reputations earned and fortunes lost. Consider the great names of American magazines established during this century and the men and women who founded them or gave them great editorial vision: DeWitt and Lila Wallace and *The Reader's Digest;* Henry Luce and *Time, Inc.;* Harold Ross and *The New Yorker;* Ben Hibbs and *The Saturday Evening Post;* Norman Cousins and *Saturday Review;* Hugh Hefner and *Playboy;* even William M. Gaines and *Mad.* The story of these great magazines and their birth is well told in Theodore Peterson's *Magazines in the Twentieth Century.*

Consider the great magazine writers and reporters, those now dead or those very much alive: the Algonquin roundtable of writers for *The New Yorker,* the late A.J. Liebling, James Thurber and all the rest; the late Richard Gehman, who is represented in this book; the late Ken Purdy and all the contemporary magazine writers. Their stories are best told in their own articles and books, many cited in the Bibliography at the end of this book. Two recent books, noteworthy and valuable are *Here at The New Yorker* and *Wayward Reporter: The Life of A.J. Liebling.*

The article writer should be aware that magazines can be divided into two generally-recognizable types: the general and the special-interest.The general magazines have a wide appeal through American life. General magazines have readerships which may include teenagers, young married adults and grandparents; the editorial content offers "something for everyone," and advertisers buy space in the general magazines hoping to attract a wide potential buying audience of both sexes and ages. In *The Changing Magazine,* Roland E. Wolseley writes:

More dramatic than any other has been the actual change in

THE HARDEST PARTS

the types of magazines. The general—appeal periodical is on the way out, or at least to limited size in circulation. Gone are the giants: *Collier's, Look, Life, American Weekly, This Week, American, Woman's Home Companion*. Three other equally famous—*The Saturday Evening Post, Liberty* and *Coronet*—also died in recent years, but have been reborn under new ownership. But they have not recovered their status as leaders. At the same time as these occurrences, hundreds of highly specialized periodicals reflecting the new interests and activities of Americans in the 1970s have appeared—dealing with ecology, apartment living and snowmobiling, for instance.

The death (and rebirth) of the great American magazines of the past such as *The Saturday Evening Post* and *Life* (and the complete death of *Collier's* and *Look* and others), can be blamed on three key factors: the costs of publishing a magazine with millions-of-copies circulation and various regional editions; the rise of television as a factor in society and the rise of special interest magazines.

In the 1950s and the 1960s, publishers of major magazines such as *Life* and *The Saturday Evening Post* discovered to their chagrin that they were spending millions of dollars for printing costs, for special regional editions of their magazines, for "numbers," trying to saturate the market and reach every potential subscriber or news-stand buyer. Yet these costs were not recovered with incoming revenues from advertising. Magazine publishers were caught in an unsolvable dilemma; how to reach millions of potential readers cheaply, then how to generate millions of advertising dollars to pay for the costs of printing millions of magazines for those millions of readers.

The solution might have been simple: X dollars of publishing and printing costs is replaced by X dollars in advertising. This simple solution was negated by one major competition: television. Network television could and did replace the general magazine in reaching all facets, all geographic areas of the country and all demographic divisions of the population, quicker, easier and less expensively to the advertiser. The telling blow to the magazines and the greatest selling point to potential advertisers was: advertisers could reach X millions of potential customers cheaper through television advertising than via magazine advertising. Thus one major vehicle of mass communication (television) replaced another (the general-interest magazine.)

Yet, despite the unhappy deaths of many of the general-interest magazines, the situation in the 1970s and early 1980s *is* optimistic because of the second major category of magazines: the special-interest magazine. As American society changes, the magazine industry reflects these changes. Thus the industry appeals to special-interest groups with special-interest magazines, magazines edited, printed and published for special-interest groups.

Consider these magazines from recent *Writer's Markets: The Mother Earth News; Animal Kingdom; Cat Fancy; The Canadian Horse; Art News; Southwest Arts; The Elks Magazine; National 4-H News; Car and Driver; Custom Vans Magazine; Private Pilot, Inc.* (for small businessmen and corporate executives); *Yankee; Baby Care; Startling Detective; Gourmet; Weight Watchers; American Collector; Rock & Gem; Parachutist;* and on and on and on.

For every sport or hobby or special interest group, there is probably one special-interest magazine and perhaps an entire category of magazines.

Perhaps you receive magazines published by groups you belong to. If you join a national organization of any kind, you may discover part of your annual dues covers a yearly subscription to the national magazine.

The American consumer can't help but be deluged by magazines. Many are special interest magazines, which the consumer actively demands. Nature abhors a vacuum, the magazine industry also abhors a vacuum, the magazine industry will fill a vacuum in society with a magazine and let it "fly" to see if the sub-section of society will support it. Often this subsection of society not only supports the magazines, but supports an entire new group of magazines. One of the major success stories in the 1970s has been the growth of city or regional magazines: *Sunset; Cleveland; Texas Monthly,* one of the bright new stars in the southwest; *D* magazine in Dallas; *Houston City* in Houston; *Far West* in California; *New York; Philadelphia* magazine and many others. Thus is born a category of magazines for urban dwellers and, a whole new sub-industry for editorial staff members, and magazine writers.

In the early 1980s, there have been special-interest magazines successfully launched in the areas of: video games; and video cassettes and home-video; environmental needs such as solar heating. As new technologies enter our world and filter down to become consumer products (home computers), magazines for those devotees will likely follow. Not all will succeed; if the sub-group is too small, the magazine will fail. If the sub-group is hard to locate and approach, the magazine will fail. If the sub-group of potential readers and subscribers can be found, but no advertising can be found to support the magazine, the magazine will likely fail.

What does all this mean to the aspiring freelancer or the novice article writer? Simply this: you have, as never before, a vast cornucopia of magazines before you, all needing, *demanding,* material on a regular basis. Many of the regional or special-interest magazines pay nominal fees for articles, but, as in any business, the article writer must begin (or perhaps *should* begin) with the smaller magazines and work up into the better-paying magazines.

What are magazine writers made of? They may or may not be college educated. The writer can be of either sex—the male-action article can be written by women; the women's magazine article can be written by men. The article writer does, however, need to be able to write, if not well, at least acceptably; the writer has to have curiosity about the world; has to *like* writing and *love* reading and has to accept demanding hours. The magazine article writer should be independent, and self-starting; the article won't write itself, you have to do it. Which means you have to actively turn away from the late night TV and march to your desk and write. Many article writers are active letter writers; still others keep diaries. Article writers love the printed word in all aspects and forms. Rules of style and techinque can be learned; curiosity can't be taught. Self-initiative can't be taught; grammar and spelling can be.

Let me end this chapter by repeating: there is no better time than now for you to begin writing and selling magazine articles. There are more magazines than ever before and you can find markets for everything you write. If you work hard, read compulsively, if you are curious and care about words, articles, books and people.

Suggested readings:

Gill, Brendan. *Here at The New Yorker.* New York: Random House, 1975.

Kelley, Jerome E. *Magazine Writing Today.* Cincinnati: Writer's Digest Books, 1978.

Mogel, Leonard. *The Magazine: Everything You Need to Know to Make It in the Magazine Business.* Englewood Cliffs, N.J.: Prentice-Hall, 1979.

Peterson, Theodore. *Magazines in the Twentieth Century.* Urbana, Ill: The University of Illinois Press, 1964.

Polking, Kirk, Chimsky, Jean, and Adkins, Rose. *The Beginning Writer's Answer Book.* Cincinnati: Writer's Digest Books, 2nd rev. ed., 1978.

Sokolov, Raymond. *Wayward Reporter: The Life of A. J. Liebling.* New York: Harper & Row, 1980.

Spikol, Art. *Magazine Writing: The Inside Angle.* Cincinnati: Writer's Digest Books, 1979.

Wolseley, Roland E. *The Changing Magazine: Trends in Readership and Management.* New York: Hastings House Publishers, 1973. *Understanding Magazines.* Ames, Iowa: The Iowa State University Press, 1965.

Also recommended:

Writer's Digest magazine, monthly; *The Writer* magazine, monthly; *Literary Market Place;* and *Writer's Market,* annual listings of publications of all types.

Chapter Two

The article, part-by-part

The late Richard Gehman once wrote, about the craft of article writing, "Every now and then a writer gets a story that proves to be so much fun it makes him forget all the drudgery, all the uncooperative subjects, ... all the other things that so often make him wonder what in the name of God he is doing in the magazine-writing business."

"Sentinel at Niagara Falls" was such an article for me. In the fall of September, 1976, while living in Syracuse, New York, I read a copy of one of the Rochester, New York, newspapers. There was a short feature about the Hill family, which caught my eye. In about 10 column inches, the article told of the Hill family of Niagara Falls, Canada, who had been rescuing people and animals from the edges of Niagara Falls for decades.

It appeared to be the type of story told so well years ago by feature writers for *True* and *Argosy*. I called Niagara Falls, Canada, information and got the telephone number for Wes Hill; I called, made an appointment to see him and then began thinking of what he might be like. I made the inadvertent mistake (for all the best reasons, wondering what a hero might be like) of stereotyping him, of typecasting him, mentally. I also daydreamed that I would have a balanced article, both pro and con about him and his family. Wes Hill was nothing like I had imagined; that made the story harder for me; since I had prejudged him, I was caught mentally off-guard. I did have that off-guard psychological trap to use in the article, however, during a sub-section on his description.

Article writers may sense that they are onto a good story when the principle subject gives them more material than necessary; or spends longer than the writer suspected was necessary; or offers a tour when the writer did not ask; or makes available records or data which is crucial to the article.

I got to the Niagara Falls area early, spent an hour at the typical tourist sites and took essentially "snapshot photos" of the Falls. I toured some of the nickel-and-dime museums, to re-acquaint myself with the Falls.

I met Wes Hill in his home; the interview lasted all day—from about 9 a.m. through the evening news. I recall leaving at or after dark. Hill gave me a tour of his basement and garage, where he had ropes and scuba equipment, showed me his power boat, took me out on the Niagara River, above the Falls, gave me a brief glimpse at the Niagara Falls, Canada

THE HARDEST PARTS

Emergency Rescue units and gave me a quick tour of the Niagara Falls, Canada Public Library, which has a special collection on the history of the Falls. I also recall he even made change for me while I used the photocopying machines at the Library.

I interviewed Wes Hill, his wife and (briefly) his children.

I eventually had an article which was not pro-and-con; it was decidedly positive, because *I liked Wes Hill* and genuinely admired (and still admire) what he stands for. Ultimately, the article writer will do best the type of articles he or she likes; on subjects which are fascinating. The article was begun in Syracuse, interrupted by a major move from Syracuse, to Austin, Texas, and finished in Austin. I sent a one-page query letter to the editors of *Cavalier* magazine; the editors responded enthusiastically and the article was sold to *Cavalier,* In this case, I didn't query first because *I knew I wanted to tackle this article.* With experience, writers know when a subject so interests them, they may forgo the usual query letter and begin the article, trusting their own judging that the article will be completed and sold to the right market.

Thus "Sentinel at Niagara Falls"...

"Sentinel at Niagara Falls"

Ernest Hemingway once described courage as "grace under pressure."
Is Wes Hill courageous?

From *Cavalier,* May, 1978

It is, perhaps, his favorite story...

Some months ago, spectators at Niagara Falls noticed that there appeared to be a dog trapped on a large rock in the rapids below Niagara Falls. The dog—a collie—remained there for two days. Others had refused to rescue it or had given up trying. The dog sensing perhaps, the dangers of the river, refused to try to leave its island. Finally Wesley Hill got his own gear and went for the dog alone.

He tied an end of rope to a tree on shore, keeping the rest of the coil in his hands. He threw another coil of rope over his shoulder like a bandolier.

"I took a few minutes to look for the light and dark places (in the river), so I could tell where the shallows were." He then waded into the river. "The rope was weighted at one end. So I'd throw it a bit upstream, pull myself out a ways with it, pull the rope in and throw it again..."

When he reached the end of the first coil of rope, he tied the second coil on, and kept going.

The Article, Part-By-Part

"I worked my way out step-by-step until I reached the dog."

He then braced himself against the rock, gently lifted the dog up and jammed the dog's hind legs into his belt, like a movie cowboy with a set of sixguns. He slid its forepaws onto his shoulders and, burdened with the weight of the dog, but able now to pull against the rope tied to the tree, Wesley Hill inched his way back to shore.

The dog, Hill says, "was just full of joy. He kissed and licked my face all the way back."

Wes Hill's story has an even happier ending. He took the dog to the nearest Humane Association and "they found it a good home, a few days later . . ."

>This is a typical anecdotal lead. After all the interview questions I had with Wes Hill, I asked him which episode he considered his favorite. He said "the dog story." If it was his favorite anecdote, it was logical to use it first. After this article was published, a reader asked me, "If this was his favorite story, as you say, why use the word 'perhaps' in the first sentence?" The answer is that the word helps give the lead a sense of conversational cadence. In this case, I tried to tell his story as if I was telling the same story to a good friend, over coffee: "Look I just met the most fascinating man. He rescues people from Niagara Falls. Lemme tell you his favorite story . . ."
>
>Article writers are cautioned to forgo the use of cliches: "like a movie cowboy with a set of sixguns," but here I wanted to use the cliche out of context, to deliberately set the scene in the readers' minds of a cowboy, legs braced, ready for a gun duel at high noon, in the middle of main street. Essentially, Hill was dueling the river and in almost the same stance. It is also best to let the subject tell his or her own story, by the use of direct questions.

Why would Wes Hill risk his life for a dog? Or a child, as he has done in the past?

>It is typical practice in newspaper journalism to ask a question in the first paragraph, to lure the reader into the story. That often has the opposite effect: it drives the reader away from the article, if the reader can't anticipate the answer to the question. Here, safely after the lead, I ask a question that I hope is in the reader's mind, at this point: *Why would Wes Hill risk his life for a dog?* His answer is something of a cliche', but still reveals the man. After his answer, summary material which capsules the theme of the article.

He says, simply, "Children and animals get into trouble because they don't know any better."

THE HARDEST PARTS

Wesley Hill is, and has been for some years, the "sentinel at Niagara Falls." The Falls and the river below, and the whirlpool below are his; he knows and understands them, like others understand airplanes, or motorcycles, or mountain-climbing.

The Niagara River, it has been said, is Wes Hill's adventure.

> After the lead, quotations and summary, comes the typical "historical middle" of the article. I had originally begun the article with the next paragraph, slightly revised to act as a lead: "From its banks and parkways, Niagara Falls is romantic, even picturesque. Honeymooners have . . ." After two versions of that lead, I knew that it might have sounded good, but something was wrong. Only after letting the drafts cool overnight, did I recall the time key: *Present—Past—Present.* When I understood that I had accidentally violated the key to most good articles. I dug through my notes to the "dog story," plugged it into the top of the story. Then the article had an active beginning, a graphic lead with a point: my original lead became what it should have been all along, the "historical middle."

Yet from the banks and parkways, Niagara Falls is romantic, even picturesque. Honeymooners have strolled at the Falls for years and years in idyllic contentment. But the rush of water is enormous and relentless: from Lake Erie, through the Falls, to Lake Ontario, the Niagara River drops 327 feet. Literally millions of gallons of water pour over the American and Horseshoe Falls every minute. The rush and cascade shakes sidewalks nearby; the mist from the Falls is constant. Below, the lower rapids and whirlpool await the innocent and helpless. Downstream, less than one mile, the whirlpool is 1,800 feet wide and one hundred feet deep. It is no less dangerous than are the Falls.

It is even a part of our language: since just after the turn of the century, a supreme example of daring, or perhaps foolhardiness, was said to be "like going over Niagara Falls in a barrel." The expression was not without truth. Many have tried to survive a trip over Niagara Falls. Almost no one defies the Falls and lives.

While this is the story of Wes Hill, the story actually begins with those turn-of-the-century daredevils who did attempt the Falls in a barrel.

In the summer of 1901, Mrs. Annie Taylor, a school teacher, tired of living on a schoolmarm's salary, decided that she would earn fame and fortune going over the Falls in a barrel. Planning her trip and the barrel took the rest of the summer of 1901. On October 4, she did enter a barrel, was towed to the center of the Niagara River and was cast adrift. The trip down the river and over the Falls shook her and knocked her unconscious. Almost twenty minutes later, rescuers on the Canadian side pulled the barrel to shore. Revived, Mrs. Taylor recovered and took to the lecture circuit. The trip somehow lost something in the retelling. She never made any money telling her story and eventually the Falls won, in a perverse way: she died penniless.

Ten years after Mrs. Taylor's successful attempt, an Englishman, Charles Stephens, decided to try the Falls. He knew that Mrs. Taylor had been knocked unconscious during the trip on the Falls; he decided to strap himself into his barrel. So he did. He tied his legs to an anvil in one end of the barrel; his arms were strapped to the opposite end of the inside. Despite all advice to the contrary, he entered the Niagara River upstream. When the barrel hit the bottom of the Falls, the anvil, Stephens' legs and one arm were torn through the end of the barrel. Rescuers found one severed arm with the remnants of the barrel. On July 4, 1928, Jean Lussier, a native of Quebec, attempted the plunge over the Falls. He had designed a ball of innertube rubber and steel. The steel would prevent the ball from being crushed going through the plunge and the rubber would prevent Lussier from being killed inside the ball.

An hour after Lussier rode over the Falls, he emerged from his ball, ashore. He later lectured about the Falls and his trip and sold scraps of rubber from his ball, renewing his supply of "authentic" innertube rubber from a local gas station when he needed more. Lussier was luckier than most.

In the early 1930s, George Stathakis, from Buffalo, decided to make the Falls plunge in a barrel of wood and steel. The barrel, with Stathakis inside, survived the plunge over the Falls, but he carried only three hours' supply of air: his barrel stayed in the current behind the Falls for almost a day, before slipping free. When rescuers found the barrel, Stathakis was long, long dead.

Thus the legacy of Niagara Falls. This legacy was a constant for the Hill family, of Niagara Falls, Canada.

> Thus the "historical middle." This was compiled from at least six or eight books about the Falls and several pamphlets. In general the rule is: assimilate historical material and re-tell in your own style. Give direct credit where credit is due and where material can only be obtained from one source. Try not to cite one magazine in an article which will be published in another magazine. An exception would be: if the original magazine is from another country, then the second magazine would have no objections. Their readers would be unlikely to have seen the original article. Remember the old wry-on-the-rocks rule: stealing from one source is plagarism; stealing from 20 sources is scholarship.

William "Red" Hill, now dead, his sons, Wesley, Major, Norman, and

THE HARDEST PARTS

William "Red Jr.," all contributed to make the name Hill synonymous with the words "courage" and "rescue."

Well before the turn of the century, Red Hill Sr., Wesley Hill's father, ran through a burning house to wake his sister and save her from the flames. He was nine at the time. The Hill family began earely to fish and take boats out into the run below the Falls. In 1912, at the age of twenty-five, Red Hill Sr. won a Royal Canadian Humane Association medal for leading twenty-three tourists to safety when ice in the frozen Niagara River broke around them. In 1918, he was again decorated for rescuing two men trapped in a boat at the edge of the river above Horseshoe Falls. Twenty years after that, he was again decorated for rescuing thousands of wild birds which had become trapped on the ice near the Falls.

Fascinated by the stories of the Falls and the lower rapids, Red Sr. made three attempts to shoot the lower rapids in a barrel. He tried—successfully—in 1910, again in 1920 and again in 1930. He eventually rescued twenty-eight people from death near the Falls and located 177 bodies—suicides and accident victims who were never reached in time.

In 1925, Red Sr. swam across the river between the Canadian and American sides in eleven minutes flat. But his last try to shoot the rapids of the river was almost a disaster. His barrel got caught in the rapids and spun helplessly in the middle of the rapids. His son, Red Jr. swam out, tied a rope to the barrel and hauled it to shore. Red Sr. vowed, from that moment on, never to again tempt the river.

> An aside of interest to writers but not germaine to readers was the fact that in the Wes Hill home, Hill had an old roll-top desk in his basement. The desk was literally—not figuratively, but literally—crammed full of newspaper clippings: "Hill Family in Another Falls Rescue" would be a typical headline. Members of the family cut and saved all the clippings they could find, but *cut off all the dates.* Many of the anecdotes, including the "dog story" don't have the requisite dates because neither Hill nor his wife could recall when they took place.
>
> Thus the vague "some months ago" in the lead episode.

His sons didn't heed their father's advice. Red Jr. twice swam successfully from the base of the American Falls to the Canadian side. Twice he conquered the lower rapids in a barrel.

Like his Father, Red, Jr. also won an award from the Canadian Society for the Prevention of Cruelty of Animals for saving deer which had been chased into the river by dogs. But on August 5, 1951, Red Jr. cast off toward the Falls in a rubber-and-net "barrel" called "The Thing." Over 300,000 watched from the shorelines, including his mother. As "The Thing" began to pitch over the cascade, it fell apart. Red Jr.'s body, nude except for his wristwatch, was found the next day; the churning gorge had stripped the body.

Red Sr.'s son Major also shot the lower rapids four times successfully, then just barely survived a fifth try at the whirlpool. Attempting another unique sport, Major made a parachute jump and landed so badly that one leg was broken. Eventually it had to be amputated. He died in 1974.

Working for the Canadian electrical utility, Ontario Hydro, Norman was killed in 1952 from falling rock inside a construction tunnel near the Falls. Apparently the shock and pounding of the Falls loosened the walls of the tunnel.

Thus, of the father and four sons, Wesley Hill remains, living and working near the Falls, on the Canadian side, in a suburb called Chippewa. Wes Hill must have mixed emotions about the Falls and the river and the whirlpool. He has seen and rescuer alike in trouble; he doubtlessly remembers vividly his own brother's death in "The Thing" and he remembers all the victims and animals he has snatched from near the Falls. As one Canadian magazine phrased it recently, "For more than half a century, his family has been almost a legend on the river, now enjoying, now challenging it, now fighting it for the lives of others who through ignorance or bad judgment, have ventured too far into its danger zone. As the last survivor of four brothers and a father who were all closely tied to it, it is only natural for Wesley to feel that the Niagara is 'his' river.

> Wes Hill told of the deaths of his family with the most amazing calmness I have ever witnessed. An almost saint-like calmness. I was so struck I recalled a quotation from Oscar Wilde "excess is the road to wisdom." Is it a cliche to think that witnessing life and death on the Niagara River has made Wes Hill wise? I think so. But I deliberately did not overwrite this. Remember: the reader is the final judge of the worth of your subject.
>
> The magazine quoted was the Abex Industries magazine, which had a front-page article about Wes Hill, earlier. In this case, I thought it would strengthen the reference if I left it "a Canadian magazine," rather than "Wes Hill's company magazine."

Wes believes that, among all the members of the family, over the years, they have been responsible for taking about five hundred bodies out of the river, usually below the Falls.

"When Dad died of a heart attack in 1942, he had taken out 177 bodies. I have helped on almost three hundred myself and my brothers helped, when they were alive. So it's a bit above five hundred now . . ."

Wes Hill works for Abex Industries, part of an industrial conglomerate. He prefers the midnight-to-morning shift, so he has more time for the river and his family. He has a blue-collar job, but given a grey suit and a

THE HARDEST PARTS

briefcase, he would have the demeanor of a statistician, or a college professor.

Life and death on the river, accidents, death, rescues, bodies, adventures, have all tempered him to an inner calmness which is impressive. He speaks slowly, and has an owlish gaze from behind his glasses. His hands are the worn hands of someone used to using rope and tools. He has a slight Canadian-English accent, pronouncing *oot* for *out* and *a-boot* for *about,* which is the English custom.

At this point, there is a two-paragraph description of Hill, which is almost an interruption of the narrative. I did want to emphasize that he certainly doesn't look like the hero I was imagining prior to the interview. My mis-conception ultimately helped me with the article. Since he was so un-like a hero when I met him in person, I wanted to tell that to the readers. Also: his accent: the slow, soft Canadian version of Great Britain-English. *oot* for *out, a-boot* for *about.* I was struck most, at his hands, and his eyes. Hands deeply groved by industrial wire and a sideways gaze, a very owlish gaze from behind glasses the thickness (figuratively) of Coca-Cola bottles. And now, inserted into the text, further, logical questions: *would you ever go over the Falls? Could you do it? How?*

The river below Niagara Falls is controlled by Canadian authorities. Wes Hill is the only individual allowed by the Canadian officials to put his own boat out on the river—and there are places even he would not go, on the river, except for emergencies.

Would he ever go over the Falls in a barrel?

"I'd never, never try it. I suspect that if I really wanted to, I could make something that would survive. A diving bell or something..." (He used the word *make* like an engineer would use the word *design* or perhaps *fabricate.*) "A diving bell would work, probably, but if I told how I would do it, sure enough, some damned fool would come along and try it..."

Stunts such as going over the Falls have been illegal for years and years, but Hill doesn't believe that will prevent people from making dangerous and foolhardy adventures. The rocks near the Falls are loose, too. That is what killed his brother, and that also makes the Falls much more dangerous.

"I don't think that's going to stop the stunting, because there's so many more people on Earth. There aren't any more frontiers and no place to go looking for gold.

"Some people are just adventure-prone. Foolish stunts are going to keep growing and growing. You can't stop people from looking for adventure; you can't stop them from dying either."

He enjoys telling the story of one man who came to him for advice on how to go over the Falls in a barrel.

"I told him, 'I'm glad you came to me first, so I'll know what you look like. That'll save a lot of time and problems when I pull you out of the whirlpool. I'll be able to identify you immediately.'

"I think that scared him off. I haven't seen him since.

"That's not too far-fetched, either. I was once called out to help with a suicide. Someone had taken his own life by jumping off the top of one of the observation towers near the Falls. It was a man I had worked with for twenty-two years. What was left of him I couldn't identify. I didn't know he was a friend until I read his name in the papers . . ."

He paused, thinking of the five hundred or more bodies that the Hill family has taken out of the river. "If they are above the Falls, it's a rescue," he says, "if it's below the Falls, it's always a body *recovery* . . ." His emphasis on the word recovery made the difference obvious. "No one survives the Falls," he says.

Nearly twenty years ago, Wes Hill decided he ought to know something about the then-new sport of scuba diving. He went about it in the forthright way he does everything; he read a book about it and then bought equipment and taught himself what he had read. Eventually, Wes led the only underwater recovery squad within forty miles of the Falls.

He became a member of the Canadian Emergency Measures Organization (similar to the American Civil Defense), and he is now the squad leader of the Niagara Falls water recovery squad. His knowledge of scuba has helped during a number of rescues. His advice alone, saved one man's life.

> An anecdote which I didn't use, but should have: Wes Hill's hobby is going out in a power boat, *alone*, and weighted with lead belts so he will neither fully float nor fully sink, Hill drops to the bottom and lets the current tumble him upside down, along the river bottom. A dangerous hobby? Apparently he doesn't think so. I'd almost judge it the equivalent of skydiving without a parachute, but Hill has his own standards of safety and danger.

"They were making a movie near the Falls," Hill says. "It was called *The Mighty Niagara* and actor Richard Boone was the star. The company hired some man who had an expedition company on the Colorado River to take a barge or boat of some kind through the rapids, below the Falls. He came to me and asked, 'What are my chances?' If anything happened, he was supposed to save his own life by swimming to shore. 'Your chances are almost nil,' I told him. I gave him my scuba tank and told him to strap it to his leg, under his costume—he was supposed to be Richard Boone—and run the regulator and mouthpiece under his coat to his collar. If anything happened, he had the mouthpiece where he could reach it . . .

THE HARDEST PARTS

"I wasn't there to see it, but he got the boat about a quarter of the way through the rapids and it overturned. He was thrown under water. There was a rescue boat out of camera range and they looked and looked for him. Finally, he came up, unconscious, right beside the boat. I got to the shore just as they were reviving him. He was on a stretcher. He told them to stop. He shook my hand. 'Wes,' he said. 'I want to thank you. Your advice and your scuba bottle saved my life.'

"When he went underwater, he had just enough time to put the mouthpiece in his mouth. He was knocked out when he hit the bottom, but he had enough oxygen to make it okay. If he hadn't had any oxygen, or never got his mouthpiece, he wouldn't have made it."

Wes's adventures on the Niagara River run the gamut from the tragic to the humorous and back again.

"I was once fishing above the Falls, on the Niagara River and I saw a big American power boat stuck on a mudbar in the river. The guy on the boat yelled, 'Help me get off this mudbar, I want to go on down the Canal . . .'"

"'The *Canal?*'"

"'Sure,' he said. 'The Erie Canal. I know where I am. I've been in the Navy for eleven years. I want to go down the Canal . . .'

"I told him, 'That smoke you may think is factory smoke on the horizon is the mist from the Horseshoe Falls of the Niagara Falls. If you lost your engine hitting that mudbar, and get loose now, you'll drift right on down and over the Falls . . .'

"Just then the rescue helicopters from the American Coast Guard came over the boats and they pulled him off the mudbar and right to shore. To this day, I still think the man believes that he was on the Erie Canal."

Many of Wes Hill's adventures are not so humorous.

"I was fishing on the river above the Falls once, and saw a small bundle drift by. I thought it was a toy—a baby. A doll. The thing got stuck and drifted in a circle and a hand and arm appeared and I snagged it with a hook. It was a baby. A small baby. Dead. To this day, no one knows where it came from. No one ever reported a child missing. Nothing."

Not only once, but twice: "I was fishing below the Falls and a package floated by that just didn't look right. I snagged that one too, and it was a baby. A fetus. No one ever found out anything about that either."

Wes Hill's restraint lends weight to his unspoken belief that someone deliberately drowned both babies.

> This anecdote was told by Hill with his placid owlish gaze almost as if he was saying to me *should I tell you this?* Is this gruesome? Certainly. Ghoulish? Yes. I have always had some doubts about it. Should this be printed? Yes, of course. It is important to Hill and thus important to the story. Where in the story should this topic be used and how should it be phrased?

Should the death of these fetuses—infants—be . . . well, how should the deaths be treated? I have believed since writing this, that the treatment is about right: late in the article, so as not to risk losing the reader at or near the lead; and the anecdote should be *underplayed* rather than emphasized. Remember again: the ultimate judge of this material is the reader. The writer need not overwrite to influence the reader.

Wes Hill has been responsible for the rescue of at least fifty people, whose boats lost power and were drifting toward the Falls, or people who were drowning, or people somehow trapped either by the Falls or the river and the whirlpool. Like the men who first successfully climbed Mount Everest "because it was there," Wes Hill challenges the river and the Falls because he is there when someone needs help.

There will, eventually, be three generations of the Hill family on the river, as sentinels for the unlucky or the unwary. Wes Hill has been training his children. Son Douglas, now nineteen, has been helping with rescues and body recoveries since he was eleven; Hill's other sons, David, twelve, and Dan, fourteen, have also helped, as has his daughter, Diane, fifteen.

"Dad always said he'd like the rescues on the Niagara to stay in the Hill family," Wes says, "and I'm sure they will."

Does Wes Hill fit Hemingway's definition of courage as "grace under pressure"? Without a doubt.

In print, this article ended rather dis-jointedly, because of a technical problem. My original sub-head was deleted by *Cavalier* magazine in favor of the sub-head "Almost no one defies the Falls and lives." While that made sense at the beginning of the article, the revised sub-head left the end hanging without a prior reference. Previously, when I submitted articles, I always sent along the article with title (headline) *and* sub-head: most professionals don't bother with the sub-head because many editors consider sub-heads part of the "artwork" of the magazine. Sub-heads are used or deleted for space reasons or because of accompanying artwork with the article. In many cases, the first item to be changed when an article is accepted for publication will be the headline; thus the novice writer should not key the headline with the lead or the end of the piece. If the headline is changed the writer's orginal emphasis may be lost.

The article writer can expect three types of research: interviews, observation (on-the-screen reportage); and library research. The article writer may also have to deal with slang, the use of unconventional quotations and the use of time. Many profile articles will begin in the present, move to the distant past, then chronologically to the recent past (this area of the article I've always called the "Historical middle") then back to the present, at the end of the article. Some may also have an educated glimpse into the future ("There will always be a Hill on the river ..."). Returning to the present and returning to the same theme at the end of the article helps the writer offer a "complete package" to the reader; the reader senses the article is complete when the writer returns to the original theme and point-in-time. (Note: although this present-past-present format is usually appropriate for a profile, this is not the only format to use for article writing. Many articles begin in the past, then move toward the present, or may flash back and forth between present and past and present.)

Suggested reading:

Baker, Bob. "How to Put Perspective in Your Nonfiction." *Writer's Digest*, Dec., 1981.

Provost, Gary. "Writing and Selling the Personality Profile." *Writer's Digest*, Nov., 1981.

Chapter Three

curiosity, compulsive reading, contacts, commitment, expertise . . .
Where article ideas come from

Just as television and radio waves are literally in the atmosphere around us, article ideas are figuratively in the air all around us. To many, article ideas do not exist; for other writers, there are never enough hours in the day to begin working on new projects. Catching these ephemeral ideas demands practice. These five guidelines may help the novice catch the elusive article idea and pin it down.

Curiosity: the article writer should be endlessly curious about the world. New fads, lifestyle changes, museums, art exhibits, new products, new technologies, may all foster ideas. The article writer who is dead to the world is useless; the article writer curious about "what makes things tick," may be a good writer about watches, bombs or people. I suspect there is something of the snooping reporter in all of us: the best writers are curious about the figure behind the facade or the *why* behind the new technology.

Curiosity may well lead you to many unexpected article possibilities and unexpected friends, achievements, publications. Curiosity is a learned trait.

Note: the key here is to look for *meaning in human events.* The writer then expresses his or her emotional *opinion about that meaning.* This is true of the major magazine markets, although it may not be true of the minor magazine markets. In *Stalking the Feature Story,* William Ruehlman writes:

> Curiosity is the other side of wonder. It's the child's incessant nagging need to know, and all good reporters are possessed by it. They are forever trying to get to the bottom of things.

Compulsive reading: Most writers read and read and read. Wherever Ernest Hemingway lived—in Paris, in Cuba, in Key West, or in Idaho, he had newspapers and magazines mailed from all over the world. Many writers live in fear of missing *anything.*

Ruehlman also says:

> A writer must . . . read. Voraciously. The things others have done will serve as points of departure for his own work. He

THE HARDEST PARTS

must read the classics and the daily newspapers, slick magazines and old yellowing pulps, handbills passed out by street partisans, the backs of cereal boxes. He should look on all of his reading as not only entertainment, but important research. The work of the masters should be examined for style and form: the casual printed matter that presents itself at every turn should be scrutinized as a possible source for stories.

That is to say, from now on you are never off duty. Your mind runs on automatic pilot. In everything you see and read, you are subtly digging.

In *The Art of Writing Nonfiction,* Andre Fontaine suggests:

A writer never knows where the next idea is coming from so he makes the conglomeration of things he reads and experiences as rich as possible. Most writers I know read three or four newspapers a day, a couple of weekly news-magazines, a dozen or so general magazines, plus scholarly or professional publications in the fields they are interested in. Jack Ratcliffe, a noted medical writer, has read the medical journals for years. Bob Bendiner, an acute political commentator, regularly gets and reads the Congressional Record—an imposing task. Because universities are centers of research in many fields, many writers have their names put on the mailing lists of university news bureaus. All these esoteric sources provide new bits of information which, when combined with the writer's own knowledge of people's self-interest, may trigger an idea for a new article, television documentary, newspaper series or book.

Contacts: People all around you may foster ideas for profiles or articles—or better. Listen to what people say and how they say it—they may be bearing a valuable idea. In late 1975, my father told me, "I can't get into the local amateur radio shop to buy parts for my amateur radio set, because Citizen Band buyers are crowding amateur radio operators out of the doors." I investigated and discovered that was true. The C.B. radio boom was just beginning in 1975.

I queried several book editors about a paperback guide to C.B. radio. One editor wrote back with the usual "Thanks but no thanks . . ." letter. Ten days later, I got a second letter from him, which read "We've changed our minds. We'd like to see your proposal." I sent the proposal and got a quick contract.

My book, *Smokeys, Truckers, CB Radio & You* (New York: Fawcett Publications, 1976) had an initial printing of 100,000 copies; went back to press immediately for a second printing and back to press again before publication for a third printing. (For a total press run of 150,000 copies.) It sold 74,800 copies in two years. I later asked the editor why he changed his mind about the idea. "I take the commuter train in and out of New York City every day. I noticed that all service stations along the railroad had signs that said 'We install CB sets.' I knew then we should have a book about CB radio," he told me. I sold the book idea because I *listened* to what my father told me about the growing population of CB radio and because the book editor *watched* what was happening in the world around him.

Commitment: Many writers are committed in several ways. First, they keep a diary. That helps them clarify their thoughts. Secondly, they become an expert in some area or field, which eventually leads to authoritative articles in that area. Martin Caidin began writing about flying decades ago. To this date, he has written over 50 books; first nonfiction, then as he became more expert, he branched into science fiction, where he too became an expert. His book *Cyborg* made him famous—it was turned into the television series, "The Six Million Dollar Man." Later, a spin-off of that series, "The Bionic Woman" made him even more money. He also wrote the book *Marooned* which was made into a film.

The ultimate perhaps is Isaac Asimov, who has been called "The Great Explainer," because of his awesome output of articles and books on almost every scientific topic known plus his books on the Bible, and other subjects. To date, he has published well over 200 books, mostly nonfiction. Every book he has seems to lead to another; every magazine article leads to a series, then a book, in hardcover, then a paperback. The best of the paperback material is turned into anthologies. By then he is working on other articles. It makes me tired just to think of his output. (And he does it without a secretary or a literary agent.)

Be an expert: In a physical activity or keep a clipping file or files of specialized subjects. One parachute jump (to write about what a jump was actually like) led me to make 360-plus jumps over a period of three years; after the 360th jump, I wrote the book *Skydiving,* covering what I knew. I had kept clippings of skydiving articles from my first jump. Friends and relatives knew of my file and also sent me clippings. By the time I sat down to write a book, I had a cardboard box of clippings, articles, other books—I had my research in my corner box waiting for me before I wrote page one. The writer need not be an expert in a physical sense to write—the writer need only keep a file on subjects of interest—sooner or later that "cardboard box" of clips may turn into an article or a book. In the meantime, don't let your spouse nag you about *putting that away*—keep the files where you can find them, up-date them and keep them in your mind.

Now, how curious are you? How much reading do you do? Do you keep clipping files? Do friends know you write or are an aspiring writer? Enlist their help in areas of your interest. Let them help build your clipping files.

Suggested readings:

Baker, Samm Sinclair. "How to Choose a Subject That Will Sell." *The Writer,* May, 1981.

Casewit, Curtis. *Freelance Writing: Advice from the Pros.* New York: Collier Books (Div. of Macmillan Co.), 1974.

Dickson, Frank A. *1001 Article Ideas.* Cincinnati: Writer's Digest Books, 1979.

Everett, Betty Steele. "Article Ideas Unlimited." *The Writer,* March, 1980.

Fontaine, Andre. *The Art of Writing Nonfiction.* New York: Thomas Crowell, 1974.

Gunther, Max. "When You Need a Nonfiction Idea." *The Writer,* January, 1976.

Mayer, Suzanne. "Journal of a First Article." *The Writer,* Aug., 1972.

Olfson, Lewy. "Build Yourself an Idea Factory." *The Writer,* April, 1979.

Poynter, Margaret. "How an Article Idea Grows." *The Writer,* Oct., 1978.

Ruehlmann, William. *Stalking the Feature Story.* Cincinnati: Writer's Digest Books, 1978.

Vandervoort, Paul II. "How to Get an Article Idea." *The Writer,* May, 1976.

Chapter Four

The Progression of an Article: Externally, planning the work, Internally, structuring the article

Many article writers have difficulty in "conceptualizing" an article—what steps come first, what steps are important, what follows the *idea*, how to proceed from idea to concrete work. The following is a paradigm of the steps a writer should take to determine whether an idea is marketable. And if it is, what the logical train of thought and action is, to complete the article.

Working with the *idea*, the writer should study two important reference books. The first is *Reader's Guide to Periodical Literature*. Check under the topic to see if there have been any recent articles published, about your topic. If there have been, how could you re-slant the idea, up-date the idea, or publish in other areas? For example, assume you have discovered a fascinating woman who is quite willing to talk with you about her rare and expensive collection of antique dolls. If you look in *Reader's Guide to Periodical Literature*, you may find magazines which have run recent articles about *dolls* and *doll-making*. You may also find similar articles listed under the topic *hobbies*. There might be a possibility to sell to magazines which have published articles under the topic heading *antiques*. Let's assume you found a two-year-old article on antique china-faced dolls in *Family Circle*. But your article topic is more about the value of antique dolls and the potentially-valuable collection of dolls which many families may have tucked in attics and basements. Since *Family Circle* is a woman's-family magazine, you may find a market in other women's magazines. With that in mind, you look up *Family Circle* in *Writer's Market*.

Writer's Market lists magazines by category and an Index. *Family Circle* is listed under the category "Women's Publications," and that category lists (among others): *Bride's* magazine, *Cosmopolitan, Farm Wife News, Glamour, Good Housekeeping, Harper's Bazaar, Ladies' Home Journal, Lady's Circle, McCall's, Mademoiselle, Modern Bride, Ms., Playgirl, Redbook, Viva, Vogue,* and *Woman's Day*. Would any of these magazines be interested in your idea? Check further under the magazine listing.

THE HARDEST PARTS

Turn to another category. How about hobby magazines? Listed under Hobbies in *Writer's Market: Acquire: The Magazine of Contemporary Collectibles; American Collector; Americana; The Antiquarian; The Antique Trader Weekly; Antiques Journal; Collectibles and Antiques Monthly; Collector's News; Early American Life; Relics;* and *Women's Circle.*

While you are browsing in the library, reading through *Reader's Guide to Periodical Literature* and *Writer's Market,* look up all articles about your topic published in the last five years. Read through them and make Xerox or other photocopies of the published articles for your research file. If there have been absolutely *no* articles done on your subject in the last five years, don't despair. Rather, turn that fact into your advantage. When you write the query letter, tell your editor that *the topic fits your magazine: your readers should be interested in this subject. Your magazine hasn't done a feature on this topic, neither had any other magazine.*

Progression of an Article

Many writers have difficulty in "conceptualizing" an article—what steps come first, what steps are important, what follows the *idea,* how to proceed from idea to concrete work. The following is a model of the steps a writer should take to determine whether an idea is workable.

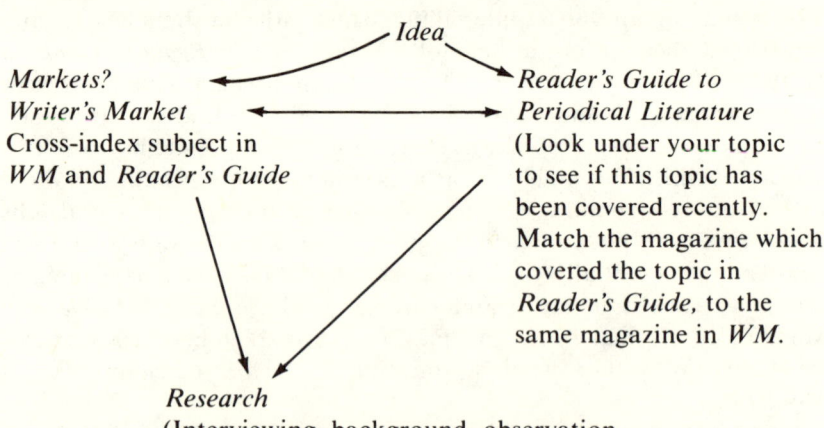

Outline
(Draft an outline, based on Intro.,
topics, subtopics, conclusion.)

Writing, Re-writing, editing
(As necessary)

*Submission to the appropriate magazine
or magazines, as required*

Let's turn to another idea and follow it through the same process. Let's assume you attend the ChiliOlympics, in San Marcos, Texas, south of Austin, which is held each September and draws chili cooks from all over Texas and assorted other "countries" like Oklahoma and Louisiana. The ChiliOlympics is a three-day celebration for rednecks and urban cowboys alike: In 1984 there were more than 320 chili teams. The event is largely for men only; women aren't allowed to be listed as "Chief Cook" in team entries or even allowed to stir the cooking chili. All right, it's chauvinistic, but many other festivals are either chauvinistic *for men only* or *for women only*. We aren't a uni-sex society yet.

Read through *Reader's Guide to Periodical Literature*. Have there been any articles about chili-cook-offs in the last five years? Look under "Cooking" and check under "Festivals." Has any other free-lancer with your idea written about Texas chili cook-offs? Which magazines are listed as printing festival articles? Cooking articles?

Since the ChiliOlympics is a men-only event, check in *Writer's Market* under "Men's Publications." There you'll find listed (among others): *Adam; Affair; Argosy; Beaver; Cavalier; Chic; Club; Dapper; Gent; Nugget; Escapade; Esquire; Fling; Gallery; Gentlemen's Quarterly; Hustler; Knight; Man to Man; Mr.; Sir; Oui; Penthouse; Playboy; Screw;* and *Swank*.

After you have done your preliminary market survey, begin the research for the article. Done *some* of the interviewing, enough to give you some idea of the slant, and scope of the article, and enough to give you some anecdotes. At this point, put down the researching momentarily and write . . .

The Query Letter. The query letter should contain some anecdotes, some quotations and should specify why the article is important to the magazine and why readers should be interested in your topic. If the topic hasn't been covered before, say so. That's a good selling point for you. Indicate tentative title and word length. Cite some of the anecdotes and research you have. (More about this in the chapter on Query Letters.)

After the query letter is written, construct an outline. The outline should list the lead; the anecdotes, topics, subtopics and a possible anecdote or quotation or summary material to use at the end.

Then write a first-draft of the article; re-write as necessary and edit. It's sometimes advisable to let the article "cool." Put it aside for a few days and re-read it. Where are weak points? Gaps in facts, research or logical statements? Are your descriptions clear and vivid? If you are using subtopics as personality sketches, are the people you are writing about unique? Can you visualize them?

If you are dealing with any kind of numbers, are the mathematics correct? Are all the dates right? (You don't want to say that John Steinbeck published *The Grapes of Wrath* in 1938 when, in fact, it was published in 1939.)

Is the title logical? Do the lead and the end match, to help make the article complete? Does the article end well? Does it read smoothly and professionally? Have you spelled everything correctly?

Note: Every article should have—at least—a clearly recognizable beginning (lead) middle and end segment. Re-check your article. The end should not just "dribble off the page" as many newspaper pieces do.

Freelancer William B. Hartley believes that the article writer should consider *four* elements to the article: in "Building the Magazine Article" (*The Writer,* March, 1972), he suggests: "In general ... the usual magazine article has four basic sections. Generalizations are notably dangerous, but I would suggest that most successful articles are built with a *lead, a statement of theme or intent,* the *body* of the article which supports and advances the theme, and a *conclusion."*

Hartley says that "an old nursery rhyme provides a simple illustration of four-element construction":

> Jack and Jill went up the hill
> (*Anecdote lead*)
> To fetch a pail of water;
> (*Statement of theme*)
> Jack fell down and broke his crown,
> (*Body.* The story itself)
> And Jill came tumbling after.
> (*Conclusion*)

Are there other methods to structure the complete article, from beginning to end, from page one to the end of the last page? In *A Practical Guide to Effective Writing* (Delta Books, 1965), Jerome H. Perlmutter suggests (among others) three key techniques appropriate to article writing: the *chronological* or *time* structure; the *simple-to-complex* structure and the *problem-to-solution* structure.

In the chronological organization, the writer structures the article in *diary* format, beginning, as Perlmutter writes, "with the first step or earliest date, and continuing to the second, third, fourth, fifth, etc. It's good to trace history, to describe the growth of an organization or process, and for similar subjects." Some writers would begin this structure after the lead, others might begin the article with this structure and include the first, or earliest segment as the lead. The chronological or diary form is useful in "A Day in the Life of . . ." articles or articles which chronicle a lengthy rock concert or similar event.

In the *simple-to-complex* structure, the writer begins with the easiest to understand idea, then brings the reader more complex and more involved material. An article of this type might begin with one family's budget, then lead into an analysis of the annual federal budget. Or a similar article might begin with one individual case of the flu, then discuss flu-type outbreaks on a national or global level.

In a *problem-to-solution* structure, the writer begins with a problem and—through the article—traces possible solutions, stumbling blocks, dead-ends and eventually the right solution or a glimpse at the right solution if it is in the future.

An example of this structuring might be: there is a new national organization, Mothers Against Drunk Drivers (M.A.D.D.): a problem-to-solution structure might show M.A.D.D. members in your state attempting to lobby your state legislature to change the state laws to lower traffic deaths which resulted from drinking and driving. This problem-to-solution structure is obviously appropriate for "how-to" articles: how to build a patio, how to knit, and so on.

Another recognizable structure might be titled the *newsmagazine profile* structure. This structure, used over and over by *Time* and *Newsweek* when they feature an individual on the cover is this:

News lead (why the individual is in the news)
to
Individual's distant past
to
Recent past
to
Present

This is a variation of the chronological structure.

Another structure perfectly appropriate to article writers is the *mystery* structure. In this structure the article writer presents a problem, crime, personality or conflict at the beginning of the article, works through description, perhaps uses suspense, and eventually reveals the solution at the end of the article, just as a mystery novelist reveals "whodunit" at the end of a novel. If the article writer reveals the solution in the middle of the article, the reader is left with little reason to finish reading the piece. Thus an article on a multi-million dollar bank fraud would reveal the "whodunit" at the end, to compel the reader to complete the article.

The *Comparison-Contrast* structure is a variation of the Diary technique. In this structure, the writer begins with a lead which perhaps is in the past or in the present, then works through the past to the present. A then-to-now structure. An example would be: the popularity of electric automobiles in the early years of the twentieth century, then an analysis of the problems of the current development of electric cars in the 1980s. Past-to-present; comparison-contrast.

A comprehensive outline and key transition makes all these formats or structures appropriate for most article topics.

It's really a simple chain: Idea, to background checking in the library, in *Reader's Guide to Periodical Literature* and *Writer's Market* to begin research; to writing the query letters; to complete research; to writing and re-writing and editing—and then mailing the manuscript and waiting for the check that will make you rich and famous. Or semi-rich and semi-famous.

Suggested readings:

Hartley, William B. "Building the Magazine Article." *The Writer,* March, 1972.

Perlmutter, Jerome H. *A Practical Guide to Effective Writing.* New York: Delta Books, 1965.

Chapter Five

Braving the library . . . Researching the article and writing the outline

Interviewing is often a challenge: a one-on-one challenge to ferret out all the information, impressions, observations and facts your subject commands. Writing the article is fascinating: the writer watches the words appear on paper and can see thoughts course through fingertips to the typewriter keys and onto the page.

Before interviewing and writing lies the library—researching the article topic in general—and many writers spend three times as much effort (or more) to research as they do in writing the article.

Libraries and research simply can't be by-passed for any normal article topic in non-fiction.

Let's back up just a bit. A common question many article writers have is: *how do I know I have done enough interviewing?* That's a fair question. The answer usually comes with experience and intuition. But, given enough time, here's the best answer. If you are interviewing subject "A," ask "A" who else you should talk to. "A" suggests "B," "C," and "D." You interview each in turn and at the end of each interview, you ask each *who else* . . . "B," "C," and "D" lead you toward "E," "F," and so on. You are done with your interviewing *when you begin to hear the same anecdotes, the same details, the same stories from each.* You have mined the same experiences from all.

The editors of *Popular Science* cite this technique in their guide for *Popular Science* contributors:

> A friend of mine and a fine magazine writer put the matter of anecdotes in an interesting perspective. She said she used to wonder when to stop research and start writing. "For a while," she said, "I used the common measuring stick that when I began running into the same material from different sources, I had covered the field pretty well. Then I thought of a better way. Now I keep doing research until I have ten good anecdotes.
>
> I think that I would always wonder what that *eleventh* anecdote might

THE HARDEST PARTS

have been if I had given up searching at number 10. But 10 solid anecdotes should be enough for most articles, so if this method seems comfortable to you, fine. I'd rather work toward mining *all* the anecdotes from *all* my chain of interview subjects.

While you're interviewing, you should be observing, color, locale, and any other detail which would lend itself to your article. Use your tape recorder and take Polaroid photographs if you can afford the additional cost, just to augment your store of mental images. Or, if you are taking professional-quality photographs yourself for the article, or are working with a professional news-photographer, arrange to have the photographs developed and printed before you write. You can prop the photographs in front of your typewriter and thus aid your memory and tape recordings with the camera eye and its results.

So, we have interviews and observation. The rest is library research. Sometimes this has to be done prior to all the interviews; occasionally the writer can do the library work later, to augment interview material.

Here are a few tips. You need to know the card catalogue and the arrangement of the library shelves; there is no set system. Since libraries are designated differently, no two will have the books and archives in the same location, but almost all use either the Dewey Decimal System or the Library of Congress System (or both).

Most library patrons are familiar with the *Reader's Guide to Periodical Literature*. There are, however, other indexes which may benefit the article writer, including *Industrial Arts Index, Catholic Index* and many others. Here you begin your search for previously-published articles which will aid your research in your topic.

What other sources might you consult? In his guide, *Finding Facts: Interviewing, Observing, Using Reference Sources,* William Rivers suggests dictionaries, encyclopedias, biographical dictionaries, yearbook and almanacs, foreign yearbooks and almanacs, books of famous quotations (or specialized quotations), atlases, newspaper, magazine and television news, government publications and reference sources in specialized fields. You may need help in finding these books and materials, but a Reference Librarian can help you—especially in the area of national government documents.

Keep in mind: not all sources are accurate. All individuals are allowed to submit their own biographical material to various Who's Who-type publications, so their "given" ages may be fanciful, to say the least. *The Dictionary of American Biography* lists only notable *dead* Americans, so your research on someone very much alive will be fruitless if you are looking in the D.A.B.

When *you know what you need—phrase the search as a specific question, not a vague generality.* Don't be afraid to consult a reference librarian—in fact, it's a good idea to cultivate the best librarian you can find and become acquaintances. Let the librarian help you—pose the search as a friendly challenge. Many librarians love to help hunt for facts and data which will turn up in articles. As Betsy Graham writes, in *Magazine Article Writing,* ". . . a professional can uncover sources you never dreamed existed. Information retrieval is a science—and sometimes an art. A great deal of it is being done by computers, but you may need help in learning where and how these services are available."

Just as during your interview, take as many notes as you need. It's a needless aggravation to try and keep five or six or seven "call numbers" in memory only to discover that you have forgotten the specific numbers by the time you have reached the stacks from the card catalogue.

Don't be afraid to ask for help getting material from inter-library loan programs. Sometimes you will have to pay mailing costs, other times the library will absorb the mailing costs. Consider the time you have—and the mails. If you have a one-week deadline, getting material from the Bangor, Maine, library to the public library in Denver or San Diego may take too long. But if you have a long-term project in the preliminary stages, don't be afraid to ask a librarian for help in obtaining inter-library loan material. Many major university libraries have complete departments solely for inter-library loans. If you have a choice in your city or town between a public library and a university library, go to the university library and use it for inter-library loan programs: college or university libraries are usually better equipped for this service.

Major college and university libraries can also obtain copies of masters theses and Ph.D. dissertations which also may be helpful. Many dissertations are unreadable (and unread when submitted by the degree candidate) but you can confirm primary sources: you can dig where the student-scholar dug for facts. Check your source-bibliography against the thesis or dissertation to confirm your complete source file. (University Microfilms in Ann Arbor, Michigan, is the largest repository of completed theses and dissertations and your librarian can help you to find suitable references there. University Microfilms will, for a fee, make you a paperback copy of a complete thesis or dissertation. There is a wait—six weeks or more, but then, you'll have the bound book to add to your reference library, should you need that source again.)

The local daily newspaper usually has a morgue file; clippings on all conceivable subjects which have appeared in the paper. The larger the newspaper, the bigger the morgue. (Now called the newspaper "library.") Whether it is called the morgue or library, this can also be a source for your preliminary research. Many newspapers think of their morgue as a public institution—and it is open to all. Others have *closed morgues,* available only to staff members. With a little courtesy, you can obtain the material

THE HARDEST PARTS

you need. Take a newspaper reporter to lunch—literally or figuratively—and politely ask that the reporter pull the file you need. Or: if the newspaper has a reader-service ("Help") column, the columnist and staff may aid your research by pulling their files for you. If the newspaper has no reader-service column, or you can't find a friendly reporter to help you, go to the P.R. department of the newspaper or even write a friendly letter to the publisher, explaining you *need* the service of the morgue files and won't the publisher or staff please help? Chances are they *will* help. Newspaper executives consider their newspapers local champions of the public, and probably won't turn down an opportunity to look like a good corporate citizen. Especially if you indicate you have been a loyal and faithful subscriber.

Does your community have a local history organization? There may well be specialized libraries in your community which may not necessarily be connected with the local library. The local librarians will know how to reach these special-interest libraries.

Ultimately, the larger the personal library, the less time the writer may have to spend at the library. Professor Roland Wolseley, who was, for many years chairman of the magazine sequence at the S.I. Newhouse School of Public Communication at Syracuse University and author of two seminal books in magazine journalism *Understanding Magazines* and *The Changing Magazine*, offers these reference books as research keys for the article writer:

Webster's New World Dictionary;
Roget II;
Rodale's *The Synonym Finder;*
Webster's Biographical Dictionary and *Webster's Geographical Dictionary; Information Please,* the American almanac and *Whitaker 81,* a British almanac;
The International Year Book and Statesmen's Who's Who, also a British publication; *Gregg Reference Manual* and Fowler's *Modern English Usage,* Theodore Bernstein's *The Careful Writer* and his two later books, and John Bremner's *Words on Words,* published in 1980 and which updates Bernstein.

Professor Wolseley observes that any writer should also own specialized libraries in the field of the writer's expertise, be it writing, aviation, music, science, or any other category important to the freelancer.

Once you have completed all your library research, and all your interviewing and all your note-taking on details of observation and reviewed your tapes, it's time to make an outline. The outline is not engraved in granite: your work may take new pathways during the first or subsequent drafts, but here is the common rule-of-thumb: *the more richly detailed the outline, the easier the writing, and the better the article.*

In his 1949 textbook *Modern Feature Writing,* DeWitt Reddick wrote:

> What functions should an outline perform? If we clarify the purpose of an outline, we shall be more likely to make it achieve its goal.
>
> 1). *A good outline insures logical development of thought.* The outline permits the writer to view the structure of the whole before he begins writing. By looking at this skeleton he can make sure that each major idea has a proper relationship to the central theme.
>
> 2). *A good outline helps to secure unity.* For every article the writer should gather more information than he uses. It is important that he see clearly what to leave out as well as what to include. The outline aids in proper selection of material.
>
> 3). *A good outline aids in securing proper emphasis on the various elements.* After the author has selected his material, he still faces the task of deciding the emphasis to be placed on each of the items or groups of facts. An outline clarifies the main points to be introduced as topic sentences and indicates the material to be subordinated.
>
> 4).*Careful preparation of an outline permits the writer to consider in advance the style to be used in developing each important section.* One idea in the article, perhaps, can be presented most clearly by a narrative incident; another is complex and needs clarification by means of a hypothetical situation; a direct quotation from an authority will give greatest force to another important thought. As he prepares his outline, the writer can decide upon the literary devices for the effective presentation of each idea.
>
> 5). *An outline aids spontaneity in writing.* The preparation of an outline exercises the mind of the writer, steeps it in the material, and creates the mood for the article. Thus, when he begins to write, he will have less trouble overcoming initial inertia and will be able to move along more swiftly because he knows in advance how he will approach each section.

More than 35 years after this passage was written, Reddick's advice is still valid.

The Contributor's Guidelines to writing for *Popular Science* magazine suggest:

> Here is an effective technique that focuses your attention on the importance of quotes and anecdotes. When you sit down with all your material to write an article, go through your research files and the transcriptions of all your taped conver-

sations and put distinctive stars or marks in the margins by all good quotes and anecdotes—one color for one, another color for the other. Pull these out—either physically or by making an inventory of them—and keep them in front of you as you make the outline. Make sure that they are spotted liberally through the manuscript. Although some exposition is always necessary, make sure you do not have long, dull expository sections. They get *boring*. Break them up with good anecdotes, quotes. Even better, change them whenever possible to narration or description.

Suggested readings:

Armour, Richard. "Good References for Writers." *The Writer*, March, 1980.

Caruana, Claudia M. "A Basic Reference Bookshelf for Writers." *Writer's Digest*, Oct., 1981.

Horowitz, Lois. "The Writer's Guide to Periodical Indexes." *Writer's Digest*, Oct., 1981.

Miles, Willim E. "Article Outlines Bring Sales." *The Writer*, January, 1980.

Spikol, Art. "Nonfiction: Getting Booked." *Writer's Digest*, May, 1979.

Rivers, William L. *Finding Facts: Interviewing, Observing, Using Reference Sources.* Englewood Cliffs, N.J.: Prentice-Hall, Inc., 1975.

Chapter Six

25 tips—and then some—for better interviewing

Just like writing itself, interviewing takes time. And work. And more time. In his exceptional book *On Writing Well,* William Zinsser explains:
> Interviewing is one of those skills that you can only get better at. You will never again feel so ill at ease as when you try it for the first time, and probably you will never feel entirely comfortable prodding another person for answers that he or she may be too shy to reveal, or too inarticulate. But at least half of the skill is purely mechanical. The rest is instinct—knowing how to make the other person relax, when to push, when to listen, when to stop. And this can be learned with experience.

There are a variety of techniques and tricks of the trade regarding interviews and interviewing. Many can simply be summarized. Some rules for interviewing should be recognized by the novice writer—still others require long tenure at feature writing. These techniques, of course, are for person-to-person interviewing, which is the most common form of the interview. Other forms are the telephone interview and the mail response.

Can an article be researched primarily by mail? In some cases, the answer is *yes*. An example: while on vacation in Odessa, Texas, from the University of Texas at Austin, graduate student Del Lemon began listening to WWWE, which came booming into Odessa *from Cleveland, Ohio*. Lemon became fascinated with "The Pete Franklin Show," a late night sports talk show. Franklin, a Howard Cosell-type commentator, was, in Del Lemon's words, "a belligerent broadcaster verbally roasting anyone who dared call in and challenge the opinions of 'The Ayatollah of the Airwaves.' His moods were like that of a child—jovial and teasing one minute, then anxious and feverish the next. He became so enraged at times that he would cut the caller off in mid-sentence and ramble in a blind tantrum for the next five minutes and then welcome the next caller to the show as if he was addressing a Wednesday afternoon meeting of the Golden Circle Garden Club.

"When I returned to Austin I could no longer pick up 3W-E out of Cleveland. I used my imagination and purchased six blank cassette cartridges and sent them along with a letter of explanation to Pete Franklin, in care of 3W-E. I told him that I wanted to write an article about his show and I needed the tapes back within three weeks. I asked him to record his program and then respond to some biographical questions I included in my letter.

"I was about to give up hope when the tapes arrived about six weeks later. I got no personal response from Franklin, but his producers sent me a letter as well as about 10 hours of recordings from five different nights of the show."

Lemon learned much from the experience: "I didn't find out as much as I would have liked, but I did learn that a friendly letter was enough to get a response from this individual. I forgot to include return postage and I would strongly urge others to be sure and do this. I also believe that a personal letter will get better results than a formal, business letter. And since most people enjoy compliments, I came on pretty strong in that area. And I feel that it is also wise to tell the individual as much about yourself as possible and why you are interested in what this person does. This helps create a feeling of trust and a two-way avenue of communication."

From the most basic to the advanced, here are the key 25 or more common tips for interviewing success:

Read all you can about your subject before the interview. Ask your local librarian for help in digging material out of old files and back issues of magazines. Read all articles in newspaper and magazine form which have been published about your subject. If you can discover no prior published material about your subject, you can . . .

Prepare in advance—write down likely or appropriate questions. Try to have six or eight (or more) questions ready when the interview begins. When you have questions to ask, and the interview subject recognizes your competence, the interview should get off to a professional start.

The interview should be at a time convenient for the subject. Change your schedule to fit the subject's—don't inconvenience the subject's time to fit your schedule. If you are doing an article on assignment for a newspaper or magazine, tell your subject so. This reassures the subject that you are not just wasting time. If you are doing the piece on *spec,* hoping to sell the article later, you may face an awkward situation, if the subject says "what (publication) is this for?" A little forethought and flattery can solve this problem. You can truthfully say, "I'm risking my time now, Mrs. Jones, because I find your story fascinating. If you don't mind taking your time with me now, I'm sure we can find an appropriate publication for your story later." You might also say, "Every writer has to start *somewhere,* Mr. Smith. I'm sure you'll always like to remember that I began my career with my article about *you.*" Or, you could say "I think that there is a possibility of publishing this article in a wide variety of publications. We can narrow that choice to the most appropriate sources later."

Be prepared for a variety of responses to your questions and, especially to you, as interviewer. Most interviews will be ordinary enough; but yet, once in a while, one interview takes on additional "baggage" of psychological content. In "The Interview or The Only Wheel in Town," in *Journalism Monographs,* Eugene J. Webb and Jerry Salancik quote George A. Kelly's types of *roles* which the subject may *perceive* the reporter to be. It does little good that you are only doing an *ordinary* interview. The subject may see you:

    ... as a protector
    ... as an absolver of guilt
    ... as an authority figure
    ... as a parent
    ... as a prestige figure
    ... as a representative of reality
    ... as a stabilizer
    ... as a temporary respite
    ... as a threat
    ... as an ideal companion
    ... as a stooge or foil

Occasionally, the reporter encounters a subject for whom the one-hour interview (or longer) is the cheapest psychiatric hour available. The cliche of the hardened reporter is accurate in part, for many reporters "hear everything" during the course of their careers. I once had an interview subject tell me, *"I almost killed a man once, in a bar fight."* You may be astonished, even *appalled,* if your subject, probably without warning, offers you such a statement. If true, swallow your astonishment and use it later.

Dress appropriately for the interview. If you are interviewing the president of one of the *Fortune 500* companies, a three-piece suit would be appropriate for men; a business-type dress for women. If you are interviewing one of The Rolling Stones, jeans and a vintage t-shirt from the 60s might be appropriate. If you are interviewing Devo, an Akron-based rock 'n' roll group who dress like robots, your guess is as good as mine. Perhaps better.

Be patient. For many people, you may be the first and only person who has ever bothered to ask them for an interview. Many are unacquainted with interviewing. Bear with them as they gather their thoughts. In "The Interview..." Webb and Salancik suggest there are at least four problems regarding your subject's answers:

1). The potential source may not know the information (the reporter) seeks.
2). The source may be aware and want to tell but lacks the

THE HARDEST PARTS

verbal skills or concepts to do so.
3). The source may be aware but not want to tell.
4). The source may be willing but unable to produce the information because it is buried beyond his conscious ability to recall it.

With some prodding, the source, or subject, may be able to tell you what you need to know.

Be prepared to ask a variety of types of questions.

Ask questions in chronological order. Many subjects are tempted to say, "This is what I did in '57 . . . this is what happened in '62 . . . oh, yes, I was such-and-such in '54 . . . ." Asking questions in logical time-order helps the subject recall his or her story and also helps keep your notes logical. And helps you write the story from clearer notes.

Ask for dates. Dates supply reader reference. (Where were you when John Kennedy was assassinated? How old? Whatever happened to the class of '65? How much older or younger than that were you?) Dates help the reader to compare the subject's life story to their own.

Ask "why" questions. Why are you in your career? Why do you live here? Why do you think . . . ? This forces the subject to explain positions and past decisions.

Don't ask "yes" or "no" questions. These questions don't help much. You have seen this type of interviewing on TV's "Monday Night Football" by Howard Cosell and company: "Tell me, Terry Bradshaw, was this the greatest game you ever played?"

"Yes."

"This Pittsburgh Steeler team—is it better than last year's team?"

"Yes."

"Are you looking forward to next year's season?"

"Yes."

"Is your relationship with the coaching staff good?"

"Yes."

And so on. A short train of answers, leaving the spectator to wonder what Bradshaw *might have said,* if the interviewer had phrased all these questions as *why* questions. *Why was this the greatest game you ever played? Why might this Pittsburgh team be better than last year's? Why are you looking forward to next season? If the relationship you have with the coaching staff is good, why is it good?* These why questions force the subject to explain his position and, if the interviewer is listening, should lead to a longer chain of why questions and answers.

Don't hesitate to ask your subject to clarify a statement.

Get a telephone number for any additional small material. Confirm the subject's telephone number or ask for the number and promise discretion if the subject has an unlisted number. Remember the old daily journalism cliche: The good writer uses the telephone to save travel. Avoid a trip across town—use the phone to confirm small bits of information which may have been overlooked.

Form a chain of subjects to interview. When interviewing subject "A" ask who else should be included. If the answer is "B," "C" and "D," interview them in turn and ask each for additional sources. Finally, your "X," "Y" and "Z" subjects tell you to interview "A," "B" and "C" and then you know you have covered all possible ground. Time may prevent you from in-depth interviews, but you should know that you have covered all major points with all major sources of information. Better delay the completion of an article (time permitting) than wonder if that missing "X" subject who is out of town, might have a key to your article you have so far missed.

DO use a tape recorder. In the past, many writers wouldn't have been caught with a tape recorder. Now, most professional writers wouldn't be caught without one. In most cases, the miniature recorders are best, especially those which can be plugged into an outlet and be run on house current, instead of solely on batteries. Why are recorders indispensable? If it's as important to you to remember the *way* people tell you things as it is to remember *what* they tell you, then you must use a tape recorder. Replaying your tapes at your typewriter, you'll catch odd speech patterns, accents, nuances, jargon and even facts you missed (or missed the significance of), perhaps because other things distracted you.

Once you have a recorder, you'll soon find other, unexpected uses for it. If, say, you've written a piece that somehow has gone wrong, and you're so close to it that you can't see what has gone wrong (or where), you'll view it freshly if you read it into your recorder and then listen to it. Weaknesses will leap out at you.

When doing research, you'll find it easier to tape descriptions of people and places—and, of course, to record sounds—than laboriously scribbling in a notebook. You'll find it easier to caption photographs from recorded notes, and sometimes on the story you'll even be able to rough out your lead on tape—more quickly and cogently than at your typewriter. You'll even note down expense account items you'd otherwise probably forget.

In museums, you can whisper information into your tape recorder from display cards, and in libraries and archives you will be able, if you hold your recorder's microphone near your lips, to whisper onto the tape so softly that even people close alongside you won't notice.

If you are writing about a concert-in-progress, you can easily keep a running record of song titles and lyrics during a concert. Later you can easily use your tapes to help keep the flow of a diary-form article.

Hardly anybody nowadays minds behinds taped, especially when, thrusting out your microphone matter-of-factly, you point out that a taped interview is more complete and quicker to get than a transcribed one.

Two other obvious advantages of using a tape recorder are: if you don't write the article immediately, the material is still perfectly fresh if you go back to it later; and the tapes can be filed and kept for legal reasons (perhaps to prove to magazine editors that you do have facts XYZ on tape and statements ABC by your subject on the same tape.)

The best recorders to buy are now the Compact Cassette machines in the $35 to $55 range—with built-in microphones (you can get a hand-held one—for another $10 to $20). And a telephone pickup—also essential—costs about $2.

Avoid the moral demands of "off the record" statements. As William E. Burroughs writes, in *On Reporting the News:*

> You can be walking around with the biggest story since Moses got the Ten Commandments, but if it's not for publication, you have nothing. Journalists are supposed to sell news, so their accepting information provided it is not published or aired is like a grocer's accepting 1,000 cans of peas provided he does not sell them. It makes the whole business pointless. Most of those who deal with the press with any kind of regularity know what they say is for publication unless there is an agreement to the contrary. Such agreements are rare because reporters know that they allow sources to act irresponsibly. Character assassination is but one manifestation of the problem. "This isn't for publication, but Oliver Smelts over at Applied Chemical once spent a year in prison for check forging." More often, however, it goes something like this: "I don't want this printed, but we're going to more than double our profits in the third quarter." What, exactly, can you do with such information if you can't report it? Nothing. At best, it's just useless; at worst, it's information designed to make you eternally grateful to the person who gave it to you. Tell him that if it isn't for publication, you don't want to hear about it.

Be prepared to skip your own line of questions—your subject may wander down his or her own mental pathways to a far more interesting and valuable conclusion than you could imagine.

Don't second-guess your subject. Don't frame questions which demand an answer you might expect. Let your subject tell his or her own story. Stifle your desire to stuff your subject into a pigeonhole of your own choice.

"According to . . ." Get your subject to confirm or deny previously-published material. This helps in two ways. First (and obviously) it helps correct your own notes—clarify the record for you, eliminate confusion.

Secondly, this may generate material which can be published, to show your subject in a revealing way. Consider this part of the remarkable article "Reflections of a Cosmic Tourist: An Afternoon with Henry Miller," by Jonathan Cott, which appeared in *Rolling Stone:*

> "I was thinking of your idea of chaos as the fluid which enveloped you, which you breathed in through the gills. And of the fertile void, the chaos which you've called the 'seat of creation itself,' whose order is beyond human comprehension. And of the 'humanizing' and destruction of the natural order. And I was thinking, too, of your statement in *Black Spring:* 'My faltering and groping, my search for any and every means of expression, is a sort of divine stuttering. *I am dazzled by the glorious collapse of the world!'"*
>
> "Yes, that's wonderful," Henry says. "I don't even remember some of these things you say I've written. Read some more from your notebook."

Observe the background, location, color. Take separate notes on background material. At the end of the interview, I try to ask some "gimme questions" which "gives me a chance" to take notes about the office, background or color the location offers. These questions are of a "who do you think'll win the next Super Bowl" type; I'm not interested in the answer—I'm buying time to get all the details down. Occassionally, I'll simply say, "Your office, shop (or whatever) is interesting—may I take a look around?" I'll never fail, from a professional standpoint, to browse through subject's library. The old cliche may be true: You are what you eat. I've changed it: You are what you read. I want to know what my subject reads. Where he gets what he or she knows.

Observe your subject's speech patterns or mannerisms. Be prepared to describe him or her to the reader. In most cases, a physical description isn't just optional, it's mandatory. Once I interviewed an owner of a small Nevada airline, Rick Blakemore. He had the habit of not saying (as most of us do) "eeerrrr," or "aaahhh" during a conversational pause, but the entire sentence *"That's a hell of a note."* He did it instinctively. Time after time. I used the phrase once early in my article and explained in parenthesis why he said it. Later I used the phrase again, without explanation. A friend of his read the article and slapped his knee. "That's Rick, all right," he said, "goldarn, I get tired of that." Blakemore's phrase authenticated the article in the eyes of his friend. If I hadn't used the phrase, his friend might have liked the article, but only liked it. The tossed-off phrase meant I really knew Blakemore.

Interview in tranquility. Get the subject away from his favorite bar (he may use the bar or his den to be "on stage" in front of his friends—he may *play to them* instead of listening to you.) Get the subject away from friends, cronies, kibitzers and assorted acquaintances. Interview them separately if you need to.

Ask about P.R. material, background or other material the subject can supply. Keep a promise to return valuable material. Make Xerox or other photo copies, if possible and return the original material ASAP (as soon as possible). Your subject will be impressed with your promptness and courtesy.

Don't forget to ask about family histories and other family material.

Be aware—wary of—slang. I once interviewed a pool hustler named Omaha Fats. I asked him what he did when he wasn't playing pool. He said, "I'm a *locksmith.*" Sound good to you? It sounded good to me. I used it in the article, with suitable accompanying material. After all, both pool players and locksmiths need good eyes and good hands and good eye-to-hand coordination. I imagined he had a shop in Omaha and perhaps a van and a small "Keys Made Here" sign in the window. Later (and before publicaton) an editor asked me, "Do you know what you've written here?" Sure, I said and told him about the key shop and the sign and all of it. "Wrong," he said, "in pool a locksmith is a guy who plays against amateurs who are so bad, he can't lose. *He's got the games locked up.*" No van, no shop, no sign. But plenty of re-writing needed in that article.

Court records, divorces, lawsuits and the like are public property. You can and should look up this material. Use it if necessary.

Ask tough or controversial questions at the end of the interview. If you ask them at the beginning of the interview, you may be thrown out of the subject's office without a story. At the end of an hour interview, or two hours or three hours, your subject may say, "Well, I didn't want to talk about *that,* but . . ." If the subject gets angry at a tough question after a long, amiable interview, you may have another bit of anecdotal material to use. Or may glimpse anger just below the surface. Or perhaps hear language you've never heard before.

Ask your subject if he or she has anything to add that hasn't been touched upon earlier. The subject may be holding back valuable material because you didn't ask for it, on the assumption that if you don't ask for it, you don't want it or need it.

Don't be awed by your subjects. Your time is as valuable as their time is, and your work just as important.

David Lampe has been a freelance since the early 1950s, is a long-time member of the American Society of Authors and Journalists, and has published in a wide variety of magazines in the United States and England (as well as magazines in Europe). His credits include *The Manchester Guardian, True, Flying, Holiday, Popular Science* and *Popular Mechanics, The Reporter, The Saturday Review, Smithsonian, House Beautiful, Parade, Family Weekly* and many, many other magazines, as well as five books published in England and co-published in the United States.

Lampe suggested a final key idea which the article writer should consider during interviews, especially for a personality portrait. His idea is this: the article writer should ask mentally, *who is to gain financially from this article?* Who will benefit from additional publicity or perhaps a promotion? (The who-is-to-gain question is not referring, of course, to the writer, but to the subjects involved.) Watch those subjects carefully. Interview with a skeptical or perhaps cynical attitude if necessary. Answers to your questions may be self-serving and not totally accurate. Mike Cox, a veteran newspaper feature writer for the Austin *American-Statesman* and magazine freelancer, suggests, in this same context, "If your own Mother says, 'I love you,' go to your Father and ask, "is it true what Mom said about us?"" The naive article writer, in many cases, won't get the true picture. Be skeptical if you need be. Be hard-boiled. A questioning attitude may pay off in an article closer to the bone of truth.

Show a copy of your article to the subject of your piece or to your experts if you are writing a scientific or technological article. Even after reviewing all relevant tapes, a writer may not fully understand the processes or technicalities involved; the article may not yet be accurate. It may take a reading by the expert and a revision to make the article totally accurate.

Most professionals take the attitude, while showing a copy of the article to the subject or expert, *I'm only the interpreter. Neither of us wishes the article to be inaccurate. Please give me your response by XYZ date.* While a few people may nitpik an article to death, the deadline helps prevent needless fussing. Most subjects will give a copy of the article a fair-minded reading. *No one,* novice or professional, wants an article to appear in print with errors of fact or mis-interpretation. And, candidly, to paraphrase Winston Churchill, when you have to kill a person, it costs nothing to be polite (and show them the article).

Don't kill a good interview with a needless faux pas. In *The Journalistic Interview* (rev. ed., Harper & Row, 1972), Hugh C. Sherwood writes, "Just a few years ago, a well-known television interviewer had occasion to interview a poet who was both blind and deaf. The poet had to place his fingers on the interviewer's lips in order to decipher her questions. And one newsweekly magazine reported that the whole affair had proved unusually moving, until the interviewer made the mistake of asking the poet if he missed going out with women. Then, said the magazine, it all became downright embarrassing."

Suggested Readings:

Berger, Paul. "A Writer's Guide to Tiny Tape Recorders." *Writer's Digest,* May, 1979.

Bernstein, Paul. "Take Care of Your Tape Recorder And It Will Take Care of You." *Writer's Digest,* May, 1979.

Brady, John. *The Craft of Interviewing.* Cincinnati, Writer's Giest Books, 1976.

Burroughs, William E. *On Reporting the News.* New York: New York University Press, 1977.

Hano, Arnold. "Interviewing: It's More than a Q & A." *The Writer,* Sept., 1981.

Hensley, Dennis E. "Getting Impossible-to-Get Interviews." *The Writer,* June, 1980.

Gunther, Max. "Interviewing for Nonfiction Writing." *The Writer,* May, 1973.

Metzler, Ken. *Creative Interviewing.* Englewood Cliffs, N.J.: Prentice-Hall, Inc., 1977.

Scanlon, Paul, ed. *Reporting: The Rolling Stone Style.* New York: Rolling Stone Press/Doubleday, 1977.

Webb, Eugene and Salancik, Jerry R. "The Interview or The Only Wheel in Town," *Journalism Monographs.* No. 2, Nov., 1966.

Zinsser, William. *On Writing Well.* New York: Harper & Row, 1980.

Chapter Seven

But what did it look like?
The art of observation . . .
But I want to know why . . .
The psychology of personality . . .

What does it look like . . . ? Why do people behave the way they do . . . ? I have always considered these questions crucial to the feature article because invariably, *your reader wants to know.* The more details of description you can use in your article, the better a mental picture your reader will have. Satisfy that mental curiosity about locale, description, so you won't leave your reader frustrated at not knowing what the article is trying to say. Remember: you are the eyes of the reader: the reader is not on the scene, you are. The reader can't see what you see. Can't observe your interview subjects and can't ask them questions; you have to anticipate what the reader wants to know—and needs to know. You have to offer the small "brushstrokes," which a painter uses to fill in the minor details on a canvas. Often, these details will be exceedingly minor—a sentence here or there—but crucial. Can you summarize a personality in the lead with a paragraph and leave the reader (at least) momentarily satisfied that he or she understands the personality you have in focus?

If you can: fine. If the "brushstrokes" demands a few paragraphs or a sub-section of your article, write about those paragraphs of detail or the subsection. Fill in the gaps so your reader has a complete picture of the subject.

Consider this exchange, between two staff members of *Newsweek,* as recalled by Osborn Elliott, former *Newsweek* executive editor, in his memoir, *The World of Oz:*

> Frank Trippett, then a reporter in our three-man Atlanta bureau, recalls a classic telephone conversation with Bill Emerson in New York. Trippett was in New Orleans in April 1962 when Emerson telephoned. The Religion section, he said, was doing a story on the confrontation between Archbishop Joseph Rummel and an excommunicated parishioner named Mrs. Una Gaillot over school desegregation. The confrontation had taken place on the archbishop's lawn, and Emerson

needed just two questions answered.

"Number one," he said, "What does the archbishop's house look like? Is it wood, or stone, or brick? Is it Victorian with ivy on the walls? What kind of day was it? Was it balmy and overcast, or hot and muggy? What does the archbishop look like? Is he old and bespectacled or what? How did he walk when he came out of the house? Did he stride angrily? Or did he walk haltingly, leaning on a cane? How was he dressed? What is the walkway like? Is it concrete, brick or gravel? What do the grounds look like? Are there oak trees and rose bushes, magnolias and poppies? Were birds singing in the bushes? What was going on in the street outside the house? Was an angry crowd asembled? Or was there the normal business traffic, passing by oblivious to the drama inside? What were Mrs. Gaillot and her friends wearing? Did they have on Sunday best or just casual clothes? What happened when the archbishop confronted Mrs. Gaillot? Was he stern and silent? Or did he rebuke her? What was the exact language she used?

"Now, Emerson said, "question number two . . ."

Question Number two . . . indeed.

Here's an example of how casual browsing through the subject's office yielded an item which proved to be the key to the lead. (Writer Tim Clark found a firehat in the office of Elliot Richardson.) Clark's article, "The Invisible Elliot Richardson," subtitled "He is the only man in history who has held four cabinet-level posts. He may also be the best known, least understood politician in America," was published in the February, 1981 issue of *Yankee* magazine.

An office can tell you a lot about the person who works in it. It gets that lived-in look, a patina of personality rubbed in by long tenancy. The history of the individual who occupies that room can be found on its walls and bookshelves, the photographs on the desk, the worn spots in the carpet. After being in some offices, I have felt that meeting the occupant was almost superfluous, because his or her shape had already been defined by the space around it.

I did not have that feeling in Elliot Richardson's office at the State Department in Washington, D.C. It was a large room on one of the top floors, with a fine view across the Potomac, warmed by the level rays of the setting sun. The furniture was comfortable, the carpeting thick. But except for a few slender clues to the occupant's identity—pictures of Richardson's wife and three children crowded onto a small corner table, 19th-century prints of Boston, a high-backed blue leather chair

But What Did It Look Like?

emblazoned with the state seal of Massachusetts—it could have been the cell of any top-level bureaucrat or, likelier still, an empty office waiting for an occupant. It was a blank page.

The only remarkable object I saw was out in the waiting area, on a coat rack. It was a white leather fire chief's helmet—not displayed, but simply hanging on a hook, casually, as if its owner had tossed it there on his way in.

I asked Richardson's secretary about it. She told me the helmet belonged to Ambassador Richardson, a gift from his staff at the Department of Commerce when he was the Secretary there. Does he wear it around the office, I inquired, pen poised? He does not. Well, I said, disappointed, it must be comforting to know that, should an emergency arise, the Ambassador will be properly attired. I wouldn't know about that, she said suspiciously.

A fire helmet: for a man who has worn as many different hats as Elliot Richardson, it seems particularly appropriate. Time after time in his career, Richardson has been called into hot spots in order to put out the fire, pick up the pieces, restore order from chaos.

Your observations may result in a list, in the article, as in this list of concert-goers to Willie Nelson's 4th of July country-music picnic:

Lined up behind cyclone fences, waiting to get in, hippies and bikers, ropers (cowboys) and straights carry coolers of beer, lawn furniture, tents, sleeping bags, Frisbees, joints. Many are drinking or drunk already. Willie's security men, in blue concert t-shirts with Security across the front, guard the gates.

and:

Suntan oil, halter tops, tube tops, straw cowboy hats, fireworks going off at 9:18 a.m. Tattoos on men and women. Earrings on men, watermelons, deck chairs. A few with furniture dollies loaded with ice chest and blankets, bumping along the grass.

Your reader may need to know some small detail which you literally stumbled over:

The sun is setting over the Texas hills. The crowd does not face the west, few see the sunset. It is impossible to tell this was once a golf course. Spectators walk ankle deep in beer cans. The sun turns from red to orange. The medical helicopter has been shuttling back and forth as fast as possible. Police have been stationed at Austin's Brackenridge Hospital to prevent trouble in the emergency room.

I had been literally stumbling ankle-deep in beer cans; that was an appropriate note to make and a detail to use in my article.

Watching what's *up front* and taking notes isn't always enough. In *On Reporting the News,* William Burroughs relates this bit of observation:

> In 1969, I did a profile of Tempest Storm, the stripper, for *The Wall Street Journal.* I spent the first of three days watching her perform four times. I watched while standing at the rear of the theater, while up front in the audience, and twice from backstage. It occurred to me after a while that the curtain separated two very different worlds as effectively as if it had been a brick wall. On one side, there was a beautiful and apparently glamorous woman bathed in a spotlight and holding the undivided attention of almost 300 persons. When she left them and came out on the other side of that curtain, however, she became a lonely, unattended, tired woman who had come to New York alone on a bus and who was picking up the fake fur and other clothing she had just taken off. The contrast would not have come to mind had I not seen the show from both sides of the curtain, and it was a contrast which, to me, marked her life and the lives of others in show business.
>
> I opened the story with four grafs, set in the present, that described in some detail what the audience saw and heard—the white negligee slipping off, three musicians grinding out her theme song, the attentive audience, and the rest. But the space separating the fourth and fifth grafs, I knew, had to be that curtain. Here is the fifth graf. It is the one that set the true tone for the rest of the profile:
>
>> Then Tempest Storm, the reigning queen of a dying art, picks up her clothes, climbs to a small, electric blue and white room, and drops into a folding bed whose soiled sheet is marked with a predecessor's lipstick. She uses a tissue to mop the perspiration from her face and from under her long, red hair, while a single fan tries to dislodge thick dust and push around hot, stale air.

In their guidelines for contributors, the editors of *Popular Science* suggest that the key to articles may well be behind-the-scenes:

> One *Popular Science* writer with years of experience in observing the progress of science and technology gives these valuable hints. "One suggestion I'd like to make for a writer going to a lab or shop for a demonstration, press show, or interview is to snoop behind the scenes. When you park your car behind the lab, or on the excuse of going to the john or getting a new tape for your recorder, sneak around behind the lab or shop and see what's in the trash barrels and junk heap.

But What Did It Look Like?

Look under benches, in little sheds and cubbies. You'll almost always find burned out pieces, broken parts, things that didn't work. They can guide your line of questioning, help you make the inventor retrace his steps. He'll also marvel at your insight.

"Also, look for empty cans or boxes of 'stuff' with the manufacturer's names on them. Such a find, as, for example, many cans of GE Glyptal, plus other brands of insulating varnish, can lead to a question such as: 'Mr. . . . . , just looking at this device I'd have to wonder if you haven't encountered internal heat and insulating materials problems. What have you done to counter that?' Such questions either release a torrent of honest information or produce an instant clam-up. In short, convey the inventor's excitement if it contributes, but look out behind the building for reality.

"Another example: I covered the introduction of one new engine that I really found to be an exciting development. When I was escorted to the lab to see it they carefully draped sheets over things they didn't want me to see. What they overlooked were two skids, one with several pans of broken connecting rods, another with a box of scuffed valve lifters, which the forklift man hadn't gotten around to hauling away from the door at the back of the lab. Later, I used this as background, not specifically, but as a 'I wonder if the extra load on the engine might not require enhanced piston and rod structures . . . etc?' It opened the interview quite a bit. What I'm stressing is the importance of probing and even snooping to shake up the presentation someone has planned for your interview."

Popular Science's editors also suggest it's not just desirable to observe the unexpected, but to keep it. In a section of their guidelines under the head "Capturing—and remembering—the essence," they write:

One of the better automotive writers around, the late Ken Purdy, had a fine technique for remembering all those little details that give authenticity and realism to an article. He always took along a Minox* camera on his research trips, and fired away constantly at everything. The resultant pictures were not of publishable quality. They were meant entirely to help him remember detail. How often has it happened that you are trying to write a description of a certain lab or of the way somebody did something and can't remember just how it was? You can't remember whether someone had dark hair or light or what that piece of machinery in the background looked like.

*An inexpensive Polaroid will work just as well.—T.F.

The pictures will bring it back. In addition, they recreate as you look at them a vivid awareness and remembrance of what it was like when you were on the scene. You recapture sharply how you felt and your reactions at the time. This is valuable stuff. It gives your writing a virtuality and authority you can't get any other way. When I am taking pictures for an article, I often shoot many others I know I won't use—just for this purpose.

Another research technique I have found extremely useful: Often, when I finish research at a specific location and go outside, I will sit in the car or on a nearby bench if there is one handy and for 15 or 20 minutes dictate my recollections, impressions, observations, feelings, and reactions into the tape recorder. I describe things, dictate paragraphs that may occur to me, anything that seems to want to come out while everything is still super-fresh in my mind and I am still excited about it. These details often help to make the article graphic and alive.

But I want to know why . . .
The psychology of personality . . .

In 1979, New Republic Books published *Telling Lives: The Biographer's Art* edited by Marc Pachter. This exceptional book is a collection of essays on literary biography by some of the most-acclaimed historian-biographers today: Leon Edel, biographer of Henry James; Justin Kaplan, biographer of Mark Twain and Walt Whitman; Geoffrey Wolff and Alfred Kazin; Doris Kearns, biographer of Lyndon Baines Johnson; Theodore Rosengarten and Barbara W. Tuchman, who has won two Pulitzer Prizes—for *The Guns of August* and *Stilwell and the American Experience in China*. *Telling Lives* should be a part of the library of all article writers for the lessons it reveals about the art of biography and the psychology of individual behavior.

In *Telling Lives,* Marc Pachter writes:

> The major struggle between writer and subject is fought . . . in the area of reputation. A modern biographer may or may not choose to reveal the intimate, the amorous details of a life, but he must, if he is good at what he does, probe beneath its public, polished self. The doubts and vulnerabilities, the meannesses, ambitions, and private satisfactions that are hidden within a social personality yield him his greatest insights.

Pachter also writes that "fine biography challenges the *pose* to find the personality." (Italics added)

In his book *Literary Biography,* Leon Edel suggests:

The biographer may be as imaginative as he pleases—the more imaginative the better—in the way in which he brings together his materials—*but he must not imagine the materials.* He must read himself into the past; but he must also read that past into the present. He must judge the facts, but he must not sit in judgment.

Substitute *article writer* for *biographer* and Edel's guidelines still apply. Could observation and psychology be the key to *your* articles?

Suggested readings:

Burroughs, William E. *On Reporting the News.* New York: New York University Press, 1977.

Edel, Leon. *Literary Biography.* Bloomington, Ind.: Indiana University Press (Midland Books), rev. ed., 1973.

Elliott, Osborn. *The World of Oz.* New York: The Viking Press, 1980.

Pachter, Marc., ed. *Telling Lives: The Biographer's Art.* Washington, D.C.: New Republic Books, 1979.

Secrest, Meryl. "The Story of a Life." *The Writer,* June, 1981.

THE HARDEST PARTS

Chapter Eight

The top of page one — types of non-fiction leads:

the summary lead; the descriptive lead; the mosaic lead; the narrative lead; the anecdotal lead; the problem (or paradox) lead; the first-person (I) lead; the second-person (you) lead; the interior monologue lead; the flat statement lead; the parody lead; the simile or metaphor lead; the "false" lead; the What-Where-When (newspaper) lead; the Name-Prominent lead; the Diary-Timeline lead.

You only have one real chance to grab all the readers you can. That means in the lead, the opening episode of the article. The lead has no arbitrary length — it might be a paragraph, three paragraphs, one page to two-and-one-half pages. Your only rule, as an article writer is make the lead interesting, make it intriguing, captivate the reader — make the reader *want* to read through the entire article.

If you don't compel the reader to read through the entire article, you haven't crafted the article well enough. In this *How to Write and Sell Magazine Articles,* Richard Gehman suggests that the lead should fulfill five objectives:

1). Introduce the story gracefully;
2). Seize the reader's interest;
3). Tell enough about the subject to make the reader wish to know more;
4). Entertain;
5). Inform.

How is this done? The writer usually has a variety of possible leads which can be used. Most of the standard texts on article writing, Fontaine, Rivers and Smolkin, Gehman and Nelson list a few lead types. Here are the most common (and some uncommon) types of leads.

Note: In all cases, *the writer's material should determine the form the lead should take* and the story follows. The novice writer should be discouraged from plugging a round lead into a square article. No writer should torture material into formulae. On the other hand, if a writer is momentarily stuck for a lead, browsing through this chapter — or other books or appropriate magazines — may suggest an entirely appropriate lead, or stimulate the writer's imagination toward that perfect lead.

The summary lead . . .

As it implies, this lead summarizes or capsulizes the article topic in a few paragraphs and gives the reader a picture of the scope of the article.

In the January, 1981, *Playboy,* horror novelist Stephen King offers a non-fiction analysis of the horror film. Here are the title, subtitle and King's first six sentences.

Why We Crave Horror Movies
"the best of them prey on our fears of everyday living . . ."

If you're a genuine fan of horror films, you develop the same sort of sophistication that a follower of the ballet develops; you get a feeling for the depth and the texture of the genre. Your ear develops with your eye, and the sound of quality always comes through to the keen ear. There is fine Waterford crystal that rings delicately when struck, no matter how thick and chunky it may look; and then there are Flintstone jelly glasses. You can drink your Dom Perignon out of either one, but, friends, there is a difference.

The difference here is between horror for horror's sake and art. There is art in a horror film when the audience gets more than it gives.

The descriptive lead . . .

This lead shows the reader the locale of the article, when the article is taking place, what the area looks like. In this lead the article writer paints a picture in the reader's mind. It can be a few deft lines, a quick sketch of the area; like a sketch that a painter might make to use later when painting an oil painting, or it could be much more extensive.

Here, from the May, 1981 issue of *Smithsonian* magazine is a descriptive lead about Dumbarton Oaks, a richly elegant oasis of culture in Washington, D.C., an estate given over to study and scholarship:

Dumbarton Oaks: stately link from past to the present

Robert Woods Bliss and Mildred Bliss created an exquisite enclave devoted to gardens, Byzantine studies and pre-Columbian treasures

By Michael Olmert

THE HARDEST PARTS

The place: the heights of Georgetown, in northwest Washington, D.C. The time: a quiet Tuesday evening, approaching twilight. Overhead, the sharply angled light is scattered into softness by the translucent green leaves of early spring. The tiniest white crab-apple petals and lilac blossoms snow themselves across a high brick wall that seems to surround an entire city block. Only a teen-ager whipping a lacrosse ball against the wall questions the bucolic charm. An opening appears in the wall—a wrought-iron gate. A single motif dominates the metalwork: a gilded sheaf of wheat. Below, the words: DUMBARTON OAKS 1920.

The story of what the sheaf symbolizes and what goes on beyond that gate is one of the minor but nonetheless great stories of taste, scholarship and collecting in this century.

But more on that later. For now, there is only time to absorb the natural simplicity and calm emanating from the countless plantings that grace the garden beyond the gate. Inside this high wall, on what turns out to be 16 acres instead of a mere city block, boxwood and ivy, magnolia and holly, wisteria and periwinkle beckon—with the allure of a charmed circle. This is indeed the *hortus conclusis* ("the enclosed garden") of medieval times, cheek by jowl with the bustling capital. Only here, the garden produces not just vegetative growth, but rather an elevation of mind. The tree of knowledge is the real root under cultivation at the place called Dumbarton Oaks.

On a gently curving footpath, the visitor approaches a Georgian mansion that dominates the land's highest aspect. Behind its great double doors, the Dumbarton Oaks Center for Byzantine Studies unfolds. For a student of Byzantium—the Greek-speaking Christian civilization that endured from A.D. 330 to 1453—this is the place to be. The mansion houses the greatest library in the world specifically related to Byzantium (90,000 volumes). And a museum wing contains a world-renowned collection of Byzantine art. Included are silver and metalwork, ivories and jewelry, coins and enamels, textiles and lead seals (p. 95). In short, all the physical elements are present to constitute a major oasis for Byzantine studies. The spiritual components are supplied by the Dumbarton Oaks fellowship program, under which scholars spend up to a year working at the Center before returning to their careers in academe.

The descriptive lead is simple enough. Yet there seems, to me, to be an older-brother of the descriptive, which no other book discusses. This is not a common lead, but does exist; few writers are comfortable with it. It's called . . .

The Mosaic lead . . .

This is a much more complicated lead because the writer overwhelms the reader with impressions, sentences, descriptions, images, impressions, fragments. Like a large mosaic on a wall, the reader must pause, step back and inhale the entire picture. I suspect that the mosaic lead is an instinctive lead used when the writer "lets it all out" in a long first segment, pauses, and continues after a spacebreak or other transition. Consider the late Richard Gehman's lead segment of "She Plumb Give It All Away":

Everybody in Norfolk who knew Minnie Clarke Mangum was fond of her; in that affectionate, respectful way some Southerners affect, they called her "Miss Minnie." They knew her as a fiftyish-sixtyish spinster with a homely face and a comfortable, restful manner, with a homely voice that drawled out homely phrases in the charming, slurring style of that section of Virginia. They liked to do business with her in the Commonwealth Building and Loan Association, where she had been working for twenty-eight years, most of that time as Assistant Secretary-Treasurer. And they liked what they knew of her: that she was a regular churchgoer who practiced her Christianity all week by caring devotedly for her blind sister. What they never suspected was that Miss Minnie Mangum possessed a streak of larceny in her soul as wide as her ample back. Somewhere in that motherly bosom, like a time bomb sunk in a tub of cosmoline, a relentlessly efficient mechanism for embezzlement ticked away for two decades—and when it finally exploded on December 22, 1955, it rocked all Norfolk and scattered likenesses of Miss Minnie's soft face to the front pages of newspapers everywhere in the world.

Consider briefly, the lead for the article "The Strange Fish and Stranger Times of Dr. Herbert R. Axelrod," which first appeared in *Sports Illustrated,* by Robert H. Boyle.

Dr. Herbert R. Axelrod is the great panjandrum of the tropical-fish world. Dr. Herbert R. Axelrod—the title and full name are always run together by admirers as though they were one word—is without rival in the burgeoning world of tropical fish. Dr. Axelrod is an intrepid ichthyologist and explorer who has made more than 40 expeditions to South America, Africa, Australia, the Fijis, Indonesia, Thailand, India and the Malay Archipelago. He can, he says, recognize more than 7,000 species of fish on sight, and he has discovered hundreds of species that were lost to science for years or, better yet, were never seen before by man. More than two dozen species of fish have been named after him, and one of these, *Cheirodon axelrodi,* the cardinal tetra, is the biggest seller in the world.

It's fascinating to watch a veteran article writer work with this mosaic lead—it's like watching a concert organist playing "all the stops" and with both feet. But chances are, if a mosaic lead occurs to a novice writer, an easier lead, more simple, more direct, clearer, would likely present itself. The mosaic lead usually belongs to those writers fully in command of the craft of writing and who *are* able to play their typewriter or word processor with all stops and both feet on the pedals.

The Narrative lead . . .

This lead most closely resembles the fiction writer's art. In this form, the article writer tells a story within a story. The opening segment is, itself, a short version of the longer article. The writer comes equipped to envelop the reader with action, description and color. Despite the obvious cliche of "the crackling cockpit radio," here is a narrative lead about a little known airline, which operates in Nevada.

Using small private airplanes and flying into central Nevada boondocks crossroads you never heard of, Mustang Airlines serves millionaire Howard Hughes' employees, miners, atomic bomb scientists and even an occasional prostitute and John. It is . . .

The World's Most Fascinating Unknown Airline

The cockpit radio crackled with instructions from the tower at Las Vegas' McCarran airfield. The pilot in the small six-passenger Cessna verified his instructions and began taxiing out to the runways, dwarfed by huge United, TWA and Braniff intercontinental jets.

The Cessna gathered speed and became airborne, heading northwest, away from the glittering Las Vegas Strip. Within a few moments Las Vegas was just a blur on the horizon. The silver plane with the red bucking bronco on the tail quickly passed over the gigantic Krupp ranch, formerly owned by the German family of munitions makers, now the command headquarters of millionaire Howard Hughes, who owns six of the biggest casinos in Las Vegas, one of the Nevada radio-tv stations and countless miles of Nevada land.

Well into central Nevada within an hour of taking off from Las Vegas, the Cessna carefully skirted the off-limits area of the Nellis Air Force Range and Atomic Energy Commission Test Site. The pilot radioed for instructions and permission to land at Mercury, inside the federally controlled area. An A.E.C. engineer, wearing a security clearance badge on his lapel, climbed into the plane and the pilot took off quickly, again carefully leaving the off-limits air space of the A.E.C.

Still flying northwest, the pilot pointed the Cessna toward Tonopah and flew parallel to Route 95, the main truck route between Las Vegas and the Reno-Carson City area. Less than fifteen minutes after leaving Mercury, the plane passed Lathrop Wells, nothing more than a wide spot in the middle of the desert.

Lathrop Wells is, however, the location of The Shamrock, the closest legal brothel to Las Vegas and one of the largest and busiest whorehouses in Nevada. The Shamrock keeps six girls busy and at least one girl works all night every night.

These three disparate aspects of Nevada life: Howard Hughes' multi-million dollar investment in Nevada, the atomic testing carried on by various federal agencies and the prostitution which is legal in 15 Nevada counties furnish Mustang Airlines with a large part of its business and interests others in the airline. For Rick Blakemore, it is worth over $100,000 a year in charter flights, regularly-scheduled flights between Tonopah and Las Vegas, and other allied services, such as air ambulance work and aerial surveying, cattle drives and air rescue.

And the story of Mustang Airlines is as fascinating as any other aspect of Nevada life.

And with that short paragraph, the transition paragraph, the article moves on.

This lead is usually a great joy to use—the article writer can have great fun pulling the reader into the article with such a lead. There is one sentence of warning here: the narrative lead must be logical; it ought to fit the article *and it must come to a conclusion.* After a concluding paragraph, the writer can begin another segment of the article, but the lead must be meaningful and logical.

The Anecdotal lead...

This form of the lead shows character, shows personality, and offers the reader an idea of the personality at work. The anecdotal lead also tells a story, like the narrative lead, but this lead form shows the personality at work, in conflict, in action. It is as if the article writer is talking directly to the reader and is saying, "Lemme tell you the best story I know about such-and-such . . ." and the article writer does exactly that. The lead from "Sentinel at Niagara Falls," earlier in this book is such an anecdotal lead.

Lynn Hirschberg used an anecdote lead with a pun ending in a profile of film-maker Steven Spielberg. The article, titled "Will Hollywood's Mr. Perfect Ever Grow Up?" appeared in the July 19-August 2, 1984 issue of *Rolling Stone*.

> When Steven Spielberg was eleven, his father came home from work with a small transistor. "Son," he said, "this is the future." Steven looked at the transistor, took it from his father's hand and swallowed it.
>
> "I think it's still here," says Spielberg, pressing his ribs twenty-five years later. "I don't think the future has passed."

The Problem (or Paradox) Lead . . .

This lead form is not mentioned in any other textbook on article writing style, yet it is an easily recognizable type of lead. This is a lead which—in essay or summary form—shows a problem in a situation or group or topic; the resolution is left for the middle or end of the article. This lead should pique the reader's curiosity about how the problem or situation began, and also pique the reader's curiosity to read through the article to discover *how* the conflict is *resolved*. Here is a sample Problem or Paradox lead from *Sports Illustrated*. This was the cover story "Ram Power," under the title "L.A.'s Fight Song: We Are Not Fam-i-lee" by staff writer Barry McDermott. The sub-head read *Quarterback Vince Ferragamo is the No. 1 complainer on a Ram team riddled with discontent, but the bickering stops at gametime.* (December 8, 1980).

> That walking piece of handsome Italian sculpture, Vince Ferragamo, the NFL's newest quarterback star, is bidding to take the bickering Los Angeles Rams to the Super Bowl once more despite the distractions of a love-hate relationship with moody fans and warfare with a parsimonious front office. So far this season he has thrown 26 touchdown passes—and has been called a choker, a dimwit, a prima donna, an ingrate and a malcontent. He also might make All-Pro.

Although the following was not a non-fiction lead, this segment from the article "The Donahue Dossier," by R.D. Rosen (published in the *Washington Journalism Review* Jan.-Feb., 1982): is also a perfect example of the Problem (or Paradox) technique:

> Donahue has the relatively rare ability to appear at once

humbly fascinated by the material on his show and embarrassed to be stooping to its level. It's axiomatic among Donahue observers that the man is modest, ingenuous, condescending, and leering, all at the same time. Most people manage only two of those simultaneously. Donahue is the Lieutenant Columbo of talk show hosts, concealing his considerable skills beneath a shabby, unassuming overcoat.

The First-Person Lead . . .

This is the voice of the writer-as-participant. Usually the first-person lead results in a completely first-person narrative article. Essentially, the writer tells the reader *This is what I saw; this is what I did; this is what it means. (Or: Here is how you can do it.)*

Here's a first-person lead, by Jeanne Rollins. Her article, in the December, 1980 issue of *Yankee* magazine, was titled "All Winter in the Stern of a Lobster Boat." The subtitle was: *We asked Jeanne Rollins of Monhegan Island, Maine, a sternwoman in a lobster boat, to describe for us one of her typical winter days beginning before sunrise. Here is her reply, word for word . . .*

My stride is too short and the gloves are too big. My hands and feet get cold very quickly and I need a four-inch wooden block to help me see out the windshield. If you saw me walking down the road, just barely able to see out of my oilclothes, you would not identify me as a big, hardy Maine lobsterman. Rather, you'd probably pass me off as a back-to-nature city slicker overdressed for the weather. Despite my inappropriate physical appearance, I spend my winters as sternwoman on a lobster boat.

My day starts about an hour and a half before the sun comes up. As Steve rolls over to get another half hour of sleep, I crawl out of the warm blankets and miserably accept the fact that I have to wake up. Probably what I need at this time of the day is a cup of hot coffee. However, fearing the call of nature on the icy sea with its limited facilities, I take my misery in utter loneliness. It takes a conscious effort for me to put the morning eggs on the table instead of in the lunch bag with the sandwiches. Nevertheless, when all is squared away, I can awaken Steve for breakfast. Now when Steve wakes up, he's as wide awake and obnoxious as a playful kitten. It is fortunate that when I bite my lip to protect myself, Steve interprets it as a smile. Breakfast is inhaled while I'm still pouring his coffee, which he drinks as he pulls on his boots. His accelerated pace helps me to forget the biting cold that awaits me outside the door. I finish putting on my six or seven layers of clothes and then stiffly follow Steve. The cold always hits me with an unanticipated shock. When there is a fresh snowfall on the ground I follow Steven's path to conserve my own energy.

And so on, into the article. One of the most remarkable first-person leads I have ever read is this lead by Stephen Becker. Becker's article "On Being a Patient," first appeared in *The Atlantic Monthly*.

First I was a wizened man of ninety-five in Washington, D.C., wearing a brown gabardine suit and a Panama hat and sitting in a warm, humid greenhouse. To step outside, or smoke a cigar, was to die; but the inactivity galled, and fear was shameful, and I stepped outside and lit a cigar.

Then I was my own age, thirty-one, in a small town in upstate New York, and there was an epidemic, and our children were dying, and we could save them only by bringing wooden objects—furniture, crates, toys—to the schoolhouse. Snow fell. Soon there were no wooden objects to be found, and our children went on dying.

Then I was a helicopter pilot, and a space pilot (this was all in January, 1959), and the manager of a theatrical troupe stranded in St. Petersburg (not Leningrad; St. Petersburg). I was the landlord of a boardinghouse on the West Coast, and my tenants were drunken, aged Bohemians, and I left because there were toads in the swimming pool. I lay on a couch in Salzburg—in the house where Mozart died—begging two beautiful women for another cup of cocoa, because the cocoa was drugged, and I needed it, and I offered them money. In Mexico we played a game with the bartender, and a blue bead curtain hung in the doorway; you won the game by smoking your cigarette, and drinking your tequila, in a mysterious and secret fashion. A man said, "Do you remember my name?" Back in New Bedford I signed off the whaler after a two-year voyage, but the house I lived in was gone. I was cold. I was in command of a Canadian corvette, but they had tied me to my bunk. On the islands between New York and France I sat down to a lavish dinner with many friends, and I was wearing a white gown, bloodstained, and my arms would not move, and I was freezing. A man said, "Do you remember my name?" I was the governor's cousin, and a car was coming for me. A lady told me to stop being silly, and I swore at her, viciously. I was in a bar in Chicago with Bao Dai, and a man was saying, "Do you remember my name?"

I finally remembered his name, and eventually got to know

him fairly well. He was an intern, and he had been trying to rouse me from a week of coma. All those lovely, horrifying, claustrophobic hallucinations—many more than the few mentioned here—had come within two or three days, as consciousness nudged me. Over the next week they ceased to be deep hallucinations, and became a fitfull delirium, punctuated by my loud insistence that I be taken back to the hospital. Yes, yes, the nurses said; and I hollered some more, because here we were in Texas, or Italy, and I had to be back in the morning for a spinal tap. Sometimes my wife was there. Sometimes no one was there, and I held long conversations with I.V. bottles. But always I was cold; and often I was tied down, pinned, locked in. I wondered why.

One morning I found out. I woke up, and was calm and lucid and full of curiosity, and they told me I was paralyzed to the neck.

That surprised me. I was too depleted for feelings of shock or tragedy, but was capable of surprise and—the word seems frivolous, but is accurate—dismay. That something was wrong, I had known three weeks before: extreme weariness, explosive puffs of pain in the legs and feet, and a slack, red-eyed face. Just after the new year one of my normally efficient systems had ceased to function, and when the failure persisted I drove myself to the hospital and had myself admitted. I was, for the first time in my adult life, a patient.

That was on a Sunday evening, and I went home ten months later.

How could a reader *not* be intrigued by this lead?

The Second-Person (You) Lead . . .

In this lead, the writer talks to the reader as casually as a friend in a face-to-face conversation. Although all writers talk to the reader's inner ear, this is as if the writer in person, is saying to the reader *This is what'll happen to you; this is what you'll see and do...*

Here's a you lead, from *Sports Illustrated,* December 22-29, 1980, by T.H. Kelly. The article was titled "Where Nothing But Good Happens." The sub-head read: *There's a sport for each man, a place he guards as his though he holds no deed, a sport like Forty Crook Branch.*

If you happen to hunt a great deal or if you spend a lot of time in the woods for any other reason, there always seems to be a half section of land somewhere that fits you better than it fits anybody else.

THE HARDEST PARTS

Any number of things can attract you to a certain place. It may be that you killed a particularly difficult turkey there, or you may find a specific bend in a creek to be unusually attractive. It could be an outcropping of rock, maybe a special view or perhaps a stand of trees, but it seems that you never go to that place without the distinct feeling that you are coming home, that every tree and rock and fold in the ground is an old friend and that nothing but good things are ever going to happen to you while you are there.

Almost invariably you keep quiet about it. If, by design, you have hunted with the same man for a number of years, he will be aware of this flaw in your character—though he will never discuss it—and will respect your idiosyncrasy. If you are not a wholly insensitive and barbaric clod, you will very likely detect a similar flaw in him and return the favor.

The Interior Monologue Lead . . .

This type of lead is difficult to use, because the writer must know his subject, figuratively inside and out. The interior monologue lead attempts to summarize the thought processes or daydreams or ambitions or plans of the subject. This can't be done by guess-work. The writer must interview the subject and probe and ask *What are your plans? What are your thoughts on this, on that? What are your dreams of the future?* The writer must know of a certainty the answers to these questions, then phrase the monologue in the subject's own words, with perhaps some fragmented sentences, because we all think in split-second electronic breaks. The human mind is, after all, the most highly-complex computer ever devised; thus the interior monologue must skillfully reflect the thoughts of the subject and the thinking processes we all do *but don't think about.* Here's my interior monologue lead from "Mr. Mileti," a profile of Nick Mileti of Cleveland, who recently put together a $40 million sports empire. The monologue is usually typographically set apart from the rest of the text to indicate to the reader that this is extraordinary material:

Start with the basics. You want to help people? Work in goal-oriented careers? Plunge into risk-oriented investments with other people's money? Okay. Pyramid investments and ideas? Sure. How? Work a fourteen-hour day, month after month. Believe. Remember your past—a Sicilian peasant's son, with a name usually associated with men like Puzo's Godfather. Remember this too: The Only Alternative To Hard Work is Unemployment. Believe in the American Dream, as corny as it sounds.

(And incidentally, what would you call an outdoors magazine written in the style of James Joyce? *Field-and-Stream of consciousness.* Sorry. I couldn't resist that.)

The Flat Statement Lead...

Occasionally, the writer can begin the article with a declarative statement of what the situation is in the field of XYZ; or how this field has changed recently; or how easy it is to do ABC; or how unusual or whatever. Although this lead *appears* to be so easy as to be a cop-out on the part of the writer, this lead may well work better than a more artistic lead. And, it just may be what the article demands. Here is an example of the flat statement lead.

In the January, 1982 issue of *Better Homes and Gardens,* writer Dan Kaercher offered an update on medicine in an article titled "Medical Breakthroughs That Could Lengthen Your Life." His article lead:

> The odds of being cured of many forms of cancer are significantly higher today than they were only a decade or two ago.
>
> The director of the National Cancer Institute, Dr. Vincent DeVita says that 45 percent of the 785,000 Americans who develop the most serious forms of cancer each year can expect to live five years or longer (five-year survival is regarded as a cure). In 1955, only 33 percent lived that long.
>
> The brightest prognosis is attributed largely to potent new anti-cancer drugs—a treatment that stems from a better understanding of how cancer spreads.

The Parody Lead...

This lead twists a known theme song, lyrics, or any other type of written or spoken prose, to establish a new perspective on the subject, or to re-inforce the connection between the subject and the original (parodied) work. Here's a lead in a personality profile of black actor Greg Morris, who starred on TV for several seasons in "Mission: Impossible." The lead parodies the "voice-over" instructions used in the opening credits of "Mission: Impossible."

> His life story sounds like one of the assignments undertaken by the Impossible Missions Force:
>
> "Your mission, Mr. Morris, should you decide to accept it, is to attend The University of Iowa as a basketball player, quickly switch to a drama major, learn all you can, leave to accept several roles in stage shows, make a few scattered televison and film appearances, and quickly become one of the featured

players in one of the best television series around, *Mission: Impossible.*"

Greg Morris *did* accept the assignment and his life story is as simple as that. Greg, who plays the stoic electronics expert Barney Collier on CBS's *Mission: Impossible* did attend Iowa as a basketball player, did switch to a drama major and learned his craft quickly.

He spent three years at Iowa, from 1958-1960 and he credits the University with giving him . . .

And so on. This was the lead from "Your Mission, Mr. Morris, should you decide to accept . . ." which appeared in the *Iowa Alumni Review* magazine, Feb.-March, 1970.

The Simile or Metaphor Lead . . .

The simile compares two items using *like* or *as*. The simile lead can often be used ingeniously to establish relationships in an article.

Here, freelancer Annette McGivney uses a simile lead to show the relationship between "Mom-and-Pop" restaurants and the chain operations, which often ruin small businesses. This lead is part of an article accepted for publication by *The Chuckwagon,* the monthly magazine of the Texas Restaurant Association.

> Today's restaurant business is like a competitive game of Asteroids: the large fast food chains are successfully firing at the smaller independently-owned operations, wiping them off the screen and into bankruptcy. Like video games, the popularity of fast food is increasing tremendously while the old family-operated cafe is being trampled beneath the golden arches of giant franchises.

More often, the simile is used in the middle of an article. Here, from the article "Pig of Bronze," in *Car and Driver,* March 1982, Associate Editor Jean Lindamood describes what it is like to drive a worn-out Jeep through the midwest:

> The Pig was running better than it had in months, thanks to a major overhaul by American Motors, and since we had time on our hands we decided not to waste our final journey in it on the Interstate. Interstates are like television: they create a false sense of participation. Saying you've been to Iowa and Nebraska when you've only whizzed through on I-80 is like saying you've been to Papua, New Guinea, when you've only seen the *National Geographic* special on the tube. Or like saying you've been to Jamaica when you spent the whole time in a walled-in Club Med enclave, paying for your banana

Types of Leads, Part One

daiquiris with plastic pop beads. So when we hit the Illinois-Iowa border, we decided to find the real Iowa. We filled the cooler with beer and headed south for Highway 92.

A metaphor makes the comparison without the word *like:* "Coney Island is like hell in the summer" (simile) or "Coney Island is hell in the summer" (metaphor). The simile or metaphor lead is often elusive: the article writer must write and rewrite, edit and polish to achieve a good simile or metaphor lead. But when the result is as exceptional as Annette McGivney's restaurant-business-like-Asteroids-game simile, the result is well worth the mental effort. For the writer and the reader.

Perhaps the most famous simile lead is the first five sentences of the late A.J. Liebling's profile of Governor Huey Long, *The Earl of Louisiana,* published by Simon & Schuster in 1961:

> Southern political personalities, like sweet corn, travel badly. They lose flavor with every hundred yards away from the patch. By the time they reach New York, they are like Golden Bantam that has been trucked up from Texas—stale and unprofitable. The consumer forgets that the corn tastes different where it grows. That, I suppose, is why for twenty-five years I underrated Huey Pierce Long.

The metaphor could be a common one, or an uncommon and surprising one; the metaphor should be intriguing, fresh, alive; like any other lead, this form demands that the writer pull the reader into the article (or book) and hold the reader until the material is complete. *Keep it interesting; keep it flowing; keep it bright.*

The "false" lead . . .

Using this technique, the writer disguises the true character, or time or location, from the reader as a mild deception, to keep the reader interested in the article. An article writer may use a long lead describing what it looks and feels like to fly a biplane. The reader may be ingeniously fooled into thinking that the lead takes place in 1914, or 1916, over war-torn France, *although the writer does not offer a time or date.* At the end of the lead, the writer may reveal that the real pilot, who had just presumably shot down The Red Baron, is a 1980s craftsman, who built the airplane in his back yard to revive interest in "seat-of-the-pants" flying.

Or, a writer may show a lawman checking his guns, pulling on his boots and generally getting ready for an (implied) 1880s gunfight; at the end of the lead, the writer reveals that the lawman who is the subject of the article is a border patrolman searching for drug smugglers along the U.S. border, and the time is the present.

In either case, the deceit is a minor one and the narrative "hook," should keep the reader interested. The false lead may be a descriptive lead, or a narrative, or perhaps an anecdote lead. This lead is limited only by the writer's imagination.

The What-Where-When (newspaper) lead...

For "hard news" articles, major and minor crime, traffic accidents, airplane acccidents, fires, other disasters and many other local stories, most newspapers use the "What-Where-When" lead. Generally, this is a three-paragraph lead, with short sentences throughout. The first paragraph *summarizes* the three key elements of the story: *what happened; where it happened;* and *when it happened.* If this story involves any fatalities from accidents, their names, ages and addresses (if known) are stated in the second paragraph.

If the article involves not only fatalities, but injuries, then the injuries are stated in the third paragraph. The article is "built" in *descending order of importance* with the key facts first (at the top of the article) and other facts next, in the order of their importance. Here is a typical What-Where-When lead:

> Austin, Tx: A three-car accident at the corner of Duval Road and Blackhawk Drive late Monday night, resulted in the deaths of five persons and injuries to two others, police reported.
>
> Howard Martin, 51, of Austin and his wife Shirley, 48; Parker Leland, 42, and his sister, Bonnie Westland, 37, of Austin, and her son Peter, 17, were all killed in the accident, which police blamed on intense fog in the area.
>
> Those injured include: Matthew Hammett, 22, and Joyce Travis, 18, who were passengers in the third car involved in the accident.

Note: in some cases, the *why* of the story (why did the event happen?) is left out of the lead, to be explained later.

For this type of article, if the writer can answer these three key questions (with short answers) the lead can be quickly written.

1). What happened?

2). When did it happen? (Usually stated in the middle or the end of the first paragraph.)

3). Where did it happen? (Also usually, but not always placed in the middle or the end of the first paragraph.)

The What-Where-When lead is a "universally used" lead for all types of newspaper news articles, but is sometimes as effective for "softer" features as well.

The Name-Prominent Lead...

In this lead form, the name of the person or persons involved is more important than the rest of the article. Thus the name is placed first. This lead is appropriate for articles involving nationally famous or infamous personalities, but is equally appropriate for regionally or locally prominent persons.

Here are two examples of Name-Prominent leads:

> Washington D.C.: President Ronald Reagan unveiled a sweeping program which will "eliminate all loopholes from the nation's Income Tax forms," in a ceremony in the Rose Garden Monday afternoon.
>
> Also attending the brief ceremony were Vice President George Bush and officials of the Department of the Treasury.

> Ashland, Ohio: A fire late Saturday night caused an estimated $50,000 damage to Mayor Dwight Leland's home while Mayor Leland was dedicating a new wing of the city's jail. Police reported the fire as "suspicious—a probable arson," Sunday morning. There were no injuries in the fire.

The Diary—Timeline Lead . . .

This lead shows change or progress over a length of time, in the form of a diary. This is especially effective for trend articles. Here is the lead from an article titled "Fighting History at 'Big White U'" by University of Texas student David Teece:

> In 1946, Heman Marion Sweatt—a Houston postman with a master's degree in biology—was denied admission to law school at the University of Texas at Austin. Sweatt was not sent away because of inadequate grades or test scores; he was turned down by the University of Texas because he was black.
>
> Four years later the U.S. Supreme Court ruled against the university, Sweatt was enrolled, and state universities across the country began struggling with how to handle racial integration.
>
> Thirty-three years after the Sweatt case was settled, the University of Texas is still struggling to shake off its reputation as a rich, white kid's university. The task has not been easy.
>
> Fall enrollment figures in 1982 showed that only 3 percent of the student population at UT-Austin was black, 8 percent was Hispanic and 81 percent was Caucasian. Of a total enrollment of more than 48,000 students, only 5,210 were black or Hispanic.
>
> The university conducted a two-year study to determine how minority students perceive the University of Texas. Results of the study released in September 1983 showed that one-third of UT's black graduates would not attend the university if they

THE HARDEST PARTS

had the opportunity to choose again. Some minority students still refer to UT as "Big White U."

Chapter Nine

The top of page one — types of non-fiction leads:

Part Two:

the quotation lead; the question lead; the dual narrative lead; the unorthodox lead; the classified ad lead; the future-tense fictional lead; the shotgun lead; the historical updating lead; the historical perspective lead; the psychological lead.

The Quotation Lead . . .

This lead simply uses a quotation from the speaker as a summary of lifestyle, beliefs or situation.

Hal Higdon is a veteran free-lancer, author and editor. He is a member of the American Society of Authors and Journalists; is Senior Writer for *The Runner* magazine and contributes pieces to a variety of top magazines. Here is a quotation lead from his article, "Running Through Pregnancy," which appeared in the December, 1981 issue of *The Runner*. The article was sub-titled "Karen Cosgrove didn't take her pregnancy sitting down."

"Having a child is *definitely* harder than running a marathon," says Karen Cosgrove, straight-faced, setting her listener up, like a stand-up comic working an audience. Karen nods toward five-week-old Benjamin Michael Cosgrove, asleep beside her in a plastic infant seat. "The thing about running a marathon is, if I had felt that bad at 17 miles I would have stopped — but there's no way you can stop when you're having a baby."

The writer is cautioned here to avoid the cliche quotation — avoid anything that might appear in the reference books of "Favorite Quotations" from the Bible, Shakespeare or similar sources. The writer must use — if anything — a lead which has impact, is unique and fresh and significant. Anything else cripples the beginning of the article. Newspaper writers avoid using quotation leads because the lead often does not reveal enough of the situation for the reader to grasp. You don't want to confuse the readers; you want to capture their attention and keep them involved in the article. Pick an *exceptional* quotation, not just *any* quotation you might happen to have in your article notes or research.

The Question Lead...

This lead is suspect also; like the quotation lead, the article writer may seize on a question lead which will cripple the beginning. Here is a good question lead, from James J. Kilpatrick's essay, "In praise of Southern Autumns":

> How do we grade our autumns in the South? Like wine, I think, for in the mountains I know best—the mountains of Maryland, Virginia and North Carolina—our autumns come in vintage years. All of our Octobers are drinkable, but some Octobers are like some Burgundies. They glow with an inner fire. Such autumns are meant to be sipped—amontillado autumns, if you please, when the oaks are as tawny as sherry. Such autumns are never to be hurried.

Here, by Hal Higdon, is a narrative first-paragraph which leads to a series of questions in the second paragraph. The sub-title was "A probe into running form and its role in optimum performance." The title was "Shadows on the Wall" and the article appeared in the November, 1981 issue of *The Runner* magazine:

> Shadows danced on the wall before me as I ran on the treadmill in the Nike Sport Research Laboratory in Exeter, New Hampshire. They were cast from lights used for photography. Black dots had been placed on my calves and shoes. A camera focused on those dots. Later, film from it would be analyzed frame by frame to show me how I run.
>
> I had to come to the lab to learn more about running form. I wondered: What is good form? Can learning to look smooth help you to run faster? Can style be taught, or is it natural? What is the latest in biomechanical research on the technical aspects of running form?

Some question leads are like: *Don't you think X equals Y?* If the answer is obvious to the writer, it might not be obvious to the reader. The reader may not answer the question the way the writer intends the question to be answered *even though the writer may have the answer in the next paragraph.* I am always frustrated by such question leads as *Don't you wish you had The New Math when you were in high school?* No. Absolutely not. No thank you. *Did you know that all the paper money we print in this country, if laid end-to-end, would stretch to Venus and back?* No. I didn't know that and don't care to know that. Some questions may make the reader resentful, not appreciative of the article: *Did you know that if you bought $100 worth of IBM stock in 1947, you'd be a millionaire today?* Joe Smith did *that*. I usually say the hell with Joe Smith and all his IBM stock. See? The question lead, unless it's a remarkable lead like Kilpatrick's, may cripple the article. Chances are if the reader skips the beginning, the reader won't dip into the middle of the article and finish it from the middle to the back. *If you lose the reader with a question lead, you'll never get the reader back again.*

The Dual Narrative Lead . . .

In this lead, the writer may have *two trains of thought* at work. In a diary form, the writer may balance the daily activities of the victim of a crime, against the daily activities of a murderer:

>At 9:00 a.m., Joe Smith gets up late, has breakfast and considers what he'll do all day, for today is Saturday and . . .
>
>At 10:45, Bob Taylor buys a gun at the Handy-Dandy pawn shop, intending to rob a quick-stop food market, to get money for a heroin fix.
>
>At 12:50, Joe Smith stops at his favorite barbershop for a styled haircut and . . .

And so on, until murderer and victim meet by accident and the victim is shot. This, obviously, is applicable for crime articles, but has a variety of other uses as well.

The Unorthodox Lead . . .

This is a lead which doesn't quite fit all "normal" categories. This type of lead, which is not only unorthodox, but until you see it, indescribable as well, must somehow fit the story. Here's an example of an unorthodox lead. *Sports Illustrated* staff writer Bob Ottum determined that Olympic winner Bruce Jenner wanted to be a film star, rather than an athlete. In his article, "Hey, Mister Fantasy Man," Ottum wrote the complete article *as if it were a film script with Jenner as the handsome lead!* Here is Ottum's lead, from the November 3, 1980 issue of *S.I.:*

>FADE IN on the top of Bruce Jenner's head. A tight shot, from the eyebrows up. His caramel-swirl hair is buffeted by winds. Occasionally, the wind stops; when it does the hair falls back perfectly into its sculptured cut as if God's hand had just reached down and patted it into place. Now the camera pulls back slowly, and we see that Jenner is at the wheel of his brandy-colored 1980 Porsche 924 Turbo. The windows are down and the sunroof is open. Between the traffic lights the car hums in third gear with the purr of an engine loafing well under its potential. Jenner is wearing tan terry-cloth running shorts and a white BMW t-shirt. A gold chain at this throat bearing the numerals 73076, the date of his triumph in the decathalon at

the Montreal Olympics, catches the sunlight. He is barefoot. He is smiling.

The camera continues pulling away, up through the open car roof, rising faster and faster, and now we see that the Porsche is tooling along the Pacific Coast Highway toward Malibu. The million-dollar shanty houses and the ocean are on the left, the towering sandy cliff on the right. At this point we notice that the smog is palpable. The air is thick with smokey haze and metallic gray in hue. The air is so dense that the titles are projected right onto the smog as the tiny Porsche rolls along far below.

Cut to title:

HEY, MISTER FANTASY MAN

The credits appear in simple white lettering on the smog. Throughout, the sound track is of the Village People humming *The Olympic Hymn.*

Lewis Lapham did essentially the same thing in his article "Has Anybody Here Seen Kelly?" about the fall of a disasterous musical comedy "Kelly," which opened and closed after a single performance on Broadway February 6, 1965. Lapham's article, which appeared in *The Saturday Evening Post* and later reprinted in *Best Magazine Articles: 1966,* is written in stage directions, like a four-act tragedy. "Kelly" was exactly that: a critical and financial tragedy for all concerned.

The Classified Ad Lead . . .

A recognizable category of the Parody Lead is the "Classified Ad" lead, in which the writer uses a parodied form of the "Help Wanted," "Houses for Sale," "Wanted to Rent," or any other of the myriad of classified ads found in the daily newspapers. This is a novelty lead and very nearly a cliche, but can be used occasionally for effect. *Newsweek* used a Obituary lead the week James Watt resigned from the Reagan administration:

> Politically dead: James Watt, 45, controversial secretary of the interior from 1981 to 1983; in Washington after a brief but devastating bout of the dread disease known as Potomac hoof-in-mouth. A darling of the Republican right and a hero to Sagebrush rebels in the West, Watt contracted his fatal infection after joking about a government study commission composed of "a black, a woman, two Jews and a cripple." He never regained consciousness.

Correspondent Thomas L. Freidman used the same type of lead to describe the last days of PLO leader Yasser Arafat:

> TRIPOLI, Lebanon—Something besides the lives of guer-

rillas and innocent civilians was lost in the past few weeks of fighting between Palestinian factions. It was the essence of the Palestine Liberation Organization itself.

Its epitaph could read: "PLO—founded in Jerusalem by Arab leaders and Palestinians in May 1964. Died in Tripoli at the hands of Arab leaders and Palestinians in November, 1983."

There probably will continue to be something called the PLO, maybe even two PLOs. But what made the PLO unique was never really its organizational structure, but the concept it represented . . .

The Future-Tense Fictional Lead . . .

Article topics which involve international arms races, global weather, national food shortages, OPEC oil, or other potential international changes may suggest a future-tense *speculative* lead. This is essentially a "what if" treatment of events in the future; a *Seven Days in May* scenario of potential holocaust, international warfare or other epic events.

In this lead, the article writer approaches the narrative skill of a "thriller novelist;" the article writer sketches in the supposed tragedy in the future in a plausible, brief way, then explains how or why we are going to (or *not* going to) reach the impending catastrophe. In a sense, the article writer using this lead acts as a science fiction writer who suggests *possible* new worlds in the next century, the next year, or as close as tomorrow.

The future-tense "what if" lead must be logical, based on scientific facts or close conjecture and again, this lead type, like many other types, *must come to a logical conclusion.*

Here, in the cover article from the March 15, 1981 issue of *Scene* magazine, the Sunday supplement for *The Dallas Morning News,* staff writer Jim Poyner uses a future-tense speculative lead about a nuclear holocaust in the southwestern United States, to begin his article "Apocalypse When? The Survivalists," an analysis of those who are prepared now, to survive nuclear war with the Soviet Union.

> WASHINGTON—The Soviet Union launched twelve nuclear missiles Monday from submarines in the Gulf of Mexico in an attack on Houston, Dallas and Fort Worth, President Bush announced.
>
> The president said damage and casualty figures are impossible to determine because communications have been greatly disrupted throughout much of the country as a result of the blasts, which occurred between 10:07 a.m. and 11:21 a.m. Bush said, however, the number of fatalities undoubtedly is enormous because the cities, comprising the nation's fourth- and

fifth-largest metropolitan areas, had only twenty minutes' warning.

For this future-tense lead, the article writer may only have to do some "what if" brainstorming with the principle subjects involved in the article. It would certainly help if the article writer was knowledgeable in the current styles of paperback "mainstream" fiction and suspense film-making, but for such a short lead (Poyner's is only seven paragraphs long), only a reasonable knowledge of fictional techniques is needed.

The crucial difference between an article with a "what if" lead and a regular non-fiction article would be in the structure of the article. Instead of the traditional:

Present
(to)
Historical past
(to)
Present

the writer would work from this framework:

Future
(to)
Historical past
(to)
Present
(to)
Future

Or, another variation on the basic structure might be:

Future
(to)
Present
(which substitutes for the usual historical past)
(to)
Future and "what if" conclusion

Essentially, the future-tense speculative lead can best be used with article topics involving lifestyle changes, cults, or topics with the potential for large-scale change: taxes; gasoline prices; wars; biological warfare; inflation; depression or other similar topics.

The Shotgun Lead...

This lead begins with *multiple examples* or *multiple anecdotes* which show key areas of the article, or key facets of the subject's personality, which will be shown in greater detail later in the article. This lead begins with an A-B-C or 1-2-3 example, usually in short paragraph form. (NOTE: Ideally, the Shotgun Lead should consist of 3 to no more than about 6 or 7 short examples. More than 6 or 7 may lead the reader to wonder what the story is actually about.) Here is an example of the Shotgun lead, in a short article by Vicki Matustik, about two University of Texas faculty members, Dr. Ruth McRoy and Dr. Louis Zurcher:

> When Jill was younger, she longed to be white like her adopted parents and siblings. As she grew older, she swayed between wanting to be "more black" like her black friends and "more white" like her white friends.
>
> Beverly, born of a white mother and a black father, identifies herself as human rather than black or white. Her adoptive white family emphasizes individuality and tells her that racial differences don't matter.
>
> Roger readily acknowledges his black heritage, although is birth mother was white. His black adoptive parents have both black and white friends who encourage racial pride and identity.

All three teenage adoptees are included in a recently published book that examines self-concept and racial identity among black and racially mixed children who have been adopted by either black or white families.

"Transracial and Inracial Adoptees—The Adolescent Years" reports results of a 1981 survey conducted by Dr. Ruth McRoy for her dissertation work through the School of Social Work at the University of Texas at Austin.

Dr. McRoy, now an assistant professor of social work at UT Austin, and Dr. Louis Zurcher - .

The Historical Updating Lead...

This technique begins in the past to help explain or amplify current conditions. John Ingersoll is senior editor of *House Beautiful* magazine and has been writing about the home and buildings for twenty-five years. Here is an Updating Lead he wrote for *Scene* magazine, the in-flight magazine for Republic airlines:

"Turn Your Home into a Solar Collector"

Around 520 B.C. in Greece, the supply of wood for winter fuel was dwindling. Rather than freeze, Greek builders began designing homes to capture the heat of winter sun. Houses were opened to the south, and roof overhangs projected just enough

THE HARDEST PARTS

to block the heat of summer sun. Most houses were built of thick clay-and mortar walls which absorbed and retained sun heat, releasing the heat during cold nights.

Some 2,500 years later, fearful of dwindling fuel supplies and escalating oil and gas prices, we're beginning to build as the Greeks did. It's unlikely the Greeks called their efforts anything more than a commonsense way of keeping warm in winter. We call it passive solar design.

Of course, we've learned a little in two-and-a-half millenniums. In fact, we have enough technical knowledge now to build a house that stays warm without a furnace and cool without air conditioning, and do both with no mechanical devices such as solar collector panels. One house—the ultimate in passive solar design—has been built in Denmark; another in Saskatchewan; and a third in Massachusetts has come within $40 of requiring "zero energy."

So much for experiments. What's important is the answer to: Can you take advantage of passive solar techniques to slash fuel bills for your present house? The response is a resounding "yes."

The Historical Perspective Lead . . .

This lead type is very much like the Updating lead; but this type is the reverse of the coin. That is, this lead could be thought of in terms of the phrases *whatever happened to . . . ?* or perhaps *did you know that . . . ?* This lead type reminds me of the Barbara Streisand-Robert Redford film, *The Way We Were,* because this lead implies *the way we were.* It could be thought of as a *lifestyle change lead.*

The *historical updating* lead begins in the past, then connects the *past with the present;* the historical perspective lead begins in *the present,* then connects *the present with the past.* There is a subtle difference between the two types of leads.

Here, under the title "Ode to the Age of the Beetle," Robert J. Connors laments the death of the VW "bug." Published in *Yankee* magazine for February, 1981, here is the sub-head and Connors' first paragraph:

A new era in automobiling began in 1949 when two misshapen, noisy little cars found their way into this country. By the time the Beetle's reign ended in 1979, more than five million people had caught the Bug. And for every one of these drivers the experience of owning and operating a car could never be the same again . . .

The classified advertisements in last Sunday's newspaper tell a sad story. For the first time, the number of plain "Volkswagens" for sale is smaller than the number of "VW Rabbits," "Busses," and "Sciroccos." A cusp of some sort had been reached, and from here on, I expect, it is just a matter of time. The Volkswagen Beetle, once lord and master of the "Imported Cars" section of the classifieds, had gradually withered to a mere two inches' worth, and the future can hold only further decay for it, eventually perhaps to the "Classic Autos" section, but more probably to "Auto Parts—Used." The end of 1979 saw the last remnant of Beetleness—the bourgeois, sybaritic convertible—gone from Volkswagen showrooms, and now the spotlight is left only to the upstart Rabbit and its ilk.

The Psychological Lead...

This lead, in the hands of a master writer, uses summary or description, but adds a subtle load of psychological "baggage," to the lead. These are rare, but handsome if accomplished well. Here magazine article writer and author Gay Talese, offers a unique portrait of Joe DiMaggio, in Talese's now-classic article, "'Joe,' said Marilyn Monroe, just back from Korea, 'you never heard such cheering,' 'Yes I have,' Joe DiMaggio answered." which was first published in *Esquire*.

"I would like to take the great DiMaggio fishing," the old man said. "They say his father was a fisherman. Maybe he was as poor as we are and would understand."
—Ernest Hemingway, *The Old Man and the Sea*

The Silent Season of a Hero

- It was not quite spring, the silent season before the search for salmon, and the old fishermen of San Francisco were either painting their boats or repairing their nets along the pier or sitting in the sun talking quietly among themselves, watching the tourists come and go, and smiling, now, as a pretty girl paused to take their picture. She was about twenty-five, healthy and blue-eyed and wearing a red turtle-neck sweater, and she had long, flowing blonde hair that she brushed back a few times before clicking her camera. The fishermen, looking at her, made admiring comments but she did not understand because they spoke a Sicilian dialect; nor did she notice the tall gray-haired man in a dark suit who stood watching her from behind a big bay window on the second floor of DiMaggio's Restaurant that overlooks the pier.

THE HARDEST PARTS

> He watched until she left, lost in the crowd of newly arrived tourists that had just come down the hill by cable car. Then he sat down again at the table in the restaurant, finishing his tea and lighting another cigarette, his fifth in the last half hour. It was eleven-thirty in the morning. None of the other tables was occupied, and the only sounds came from the bar where a liquor salesman was laughing at something the headwaiter had said. But then the salesman, his briefcase under his arm, headed for the door, stopping briefly to peek into the dining room and call out, "See you later, Joe." Joe DiMaggio turned and waved at the salesman. Then the room was quiet again.

In his book, *The Art of Writing Nonfiction,* Andre Fontaine comments:

> Here Talese has said a great deal about what will be the essential message of his story. The girl, of course, is a symbol for the dead Marilyn, the fishermen, for DiMaggio, who came from a family of fishermen. The gulf between them is suggested both by the fact that she is a tourist, taking their picture and that they speak a dialect she cannot understand. Joe, watching from behind a window, suggests the distance of his loss from her.
>
> The next paragraph tells about his loneliness, his tension—his fifth cigarette in a half-hour—his reserve, his prominence and the adulation he still gets as a former great athlete. Quite a bit to get into two paragraphs.

Quite a bit indeed. I'd like to add a comment Andre Fontaine didn't mention: the *tier* effect here. In this lead, the fishermen are lowest, on the water; the girl, an *icon* for the now-dead Marilyn Monroe is above them, but as Fontaine observes, she can't understand their Sicilian dialect as they talk about her. Joe DiMaggio, higher, inside the restaurant, can neither hear the girl, if she said anything, nor the fishermen. Each is separated from the others by a physical and psychological gulf.

The tier effect is *chronological* as well as physical: The fishermen in the boats represent DiMaggio's early life; the Marilyn Monroe *icon* his middle years and the man in the restaurant the latest stages of his years.

In his book *Articles and Features,* Roy Paul Nelson suggests some of these previous types and a couple of others: *The Humor Lead* and *The Generalization Lead.* I think that I'd be very wary of humor, *especially* in the article lead. Stated simply, one person's sense of humor may be another person's ennui; something hilarious to you may fall flat to your readers. Worse yet, a manuscript submitted for publication with humor in the lead may fall flat with the editor who doesn't share your sense of humor, thus the article may be returned with the usual "Thanks, not for us" rejection slip. Since most humor is broad and obvious, but most writing is subtle and sophisticated, the writer has the odd mix of a Red Skelton-type joke in a Woody Allen-type vehicle; the two don't mix. As Pete Fountain said, when he quit the Lawrence Welk Show to play jazz clarinet in New Orleans, "Bourbon and champagne don't mix."

Nelson's generalization lead might begin: "The total dog-and-cat food sales in the U.S. last year was higher than the national budgets of 37 countries of the world, including Chile, Monte Carlo, Switzerland and the Bahamas, among others . . ."

There are, of course, infinite ways to combine these forms of leads. The interior monologue lead could end with a question. The descriptive first paragraph could end with a rhetorical question. The second-person (you) lead could ease into a descriptive second paragraph and so on. Consider John Steinbeck's epic novel *Cannery Row*. Although it is *fiction*, the techniques are the same.

Steinbeck's first three paragraphs are: the first a mosaic paragraph leads into the second, a classic paragraph of pure description, followed by a paragraph involving the second-person *you* usage and a metaphor.

Most writers thrash around when they sit down to write the lead. *Which lead should be used? Why?* Sometimes the act of beginning a story is an act of faith—the writer hopes his mental processes will produce a suitable—even exceptional lead—then the story will flow automatically. Sometimes the lead comes boiling up from the bottom of the writer's mind. In these cases the writer is thankful—even astonished. Often the search for the right lead makes the writer sharpen pencils endlessly, or throw away what seems to be reams of paper. The writer in agony over the lead could ask several simple questions: *What's the best anecdote I have in my notes? The best quotation? The best description? Is there a good comparison here? Narrative? What did I see during my research? What should the reader expect to know first? What kinds of leads does the magazine run, that I'd like to sell this to? Did I interview anyone with exceptional physical characteristics I could describe first? What highlights would I pick up by reviewing all my tapes?*

Here's a tip about leads which may work for you, from Dr. Dian Dincin Buchman, like Hal Higdon, a member of the American Society of Authors and Journalists. She says, "Oh how I struggled with my leads when I first started writing. Then a brilliant editor of *New York* Magazine, Judith Daniels (now of *Savvy*), told me a useful thing which I can pass on. 'Cut out all your first paragraphs, Dian, and start on your second!'

"That made a lot of sense (for me) and I got into the meat of the article immediately. A good lead should emanate from the context of the story. And now, instead of working for hours exploring my first brilliant words, or trying to think of an appropriate anecdote, I write the article, then find the lead. Sometimes it is an anecdote, even one that may have been told to me in the *last moment* of a long interview."

The lead is the key to the well-crafted article. Write, rewrite, edit, change, write, re-write.

Chapter Ten

Do's and Don't's of Writing Query Letters

Simply stated: *the query letter demands as much practice and attention as does the feature article.*

It does the writer little good to be an exceptional researcher, to interview carefully and comprehensively, to organize material logically and coherently and to be a professional writer *if the query letter is not sufficiently well-crafted to sell the article.*

Phrased another way: would you try to sell your automobile by description alone? No. You'd probably let a buyer peer under the hood, kick the tires, take it around the block or around town, look into the trunk and finally make a decision. Yet, the article writer has a product to sell—to publish—and the writer has to sell it on description alone—the query letter—which is sent the editor prior to acceptance of the article. Here is the crossroads between writing skills and salesmanship. You have a product to sell. *Sell it.*

Query letters take practice and re-writing. Many article writers are compulsive letter writers—I have known some to have a constant barrage of letters outgoing to friends, cronies, acquaintances and enemies. Many other writers keep personal diaries. These writers have an instinctive advantage when they sit down to write query letters.

In *Free-Lancer and Staff Writer,* William L. Rivers and Shelley Smolkin offer three basic rules for query letters:

> *Give the basics* of the story. Do this by explaining not only what the story will be about but what your sources of information will be and who you plan to interview. It is not necessary to have already done the research and interviews; it is necessary to have decided what topics you will cover and how you will do it.
>
> *Show why this is a good story* for this magazine. Use your skills as a magazine analyst to point out the relevance of the subject to the magazine's audience or how the article fits in with the magazine's editorial policy. If you have a particular department in mind for the article, say so.
>
> *Convince the editor* that you are the person to write this story. Think of the query as a short article, written by you in your best style. It is a sample of your writing that you know the

editor will read.

There are, perhaps, more guidelines than these, which can be offered to article writers.

Do make the letter one page, single-spaced. Editors have to read constantly. Help them simplify their job. Condense your idea into one page. If you send a letter longer than one page, you haven't written it well enough.

Read the magazine before querying the editor. On this point, Maurice Zolotow, who has been an author and freelance writer since 1941, says, "I have never liked to do detailed outlines and would rather write a piece on spec than do a long outline. Usually I write a letter to an editor whom I may or may not know, or whom I may or may not have worked with. I get disgusted when I hear tyros (or even pros) ask 'What are the market needs of *Los Angeles Magazine* or *Cosmopolitan* or *Reader's Digest* or whatever?' I always say, 'Why do you ask? Don't you read the magazine?' and if they say 'No,' I say, 'If you don't read it and if you don't like it, the odds are that you won't be able to write for it.' I mean not just buying a few issues of *Reader's Digest* to get an idea of 'market needs' but reading a magazine *every issue* because you love it and enjoy reading it."

Use 8½" x 11" plain paper for your letters. You are writing a business letter, not a personal note. Many freelancers have their own office stationery; that's fine, but unnecessary for beginners. A good bond paper will work just as well. You are selling an article topic, remember, not office supplies.

Address the editor by name and spell his or her name correctly. Do you hate mail that arrives in your mail box addressed "Dear Sir" or "Dear Ms." or "Dear Occupant"? I routinely throw all that away. Letters addressed to "Dear Editor" appear to be junk mail. They also show, if the editor reads them at all, that the writer is not sufficiently interested in the magazine to discover the editor's name.

Given a choice of names on the magazine's masthead, which name should the writer respond to? In general, this is the accepted order: If specialized article: Department Editor. If general article: Articles Editor; If no A.E. is listed, the Managing Editor, if no M.E. is listed, the Editor. If several Managing Editors are listed: pick one.

Curiosity and interest help sell articles. Make your editor intrigued by what you have to sell.

Summarize the article in two or three paragraphs, or perhaps the first two-thirds of the page. Use the rest of the available space to list the headline and probable word length *(even if the headline or word length may be changed during the final writing and editing).*

Offer photographs if you can take them, or may be able to have others take them for you.

Keep paragraphs short. Make your letter easy to read.

Keep the letter clean. Stylistically and physically, you want to present the best possible appearance. Poor grammar, inept punctuation, illogical reasoning or even a dirty letter or envelope may turn editors off.

Keep a copy of the query letter. As you practice with query letter style, you may wish to keep a well-crafted letter for later reference.

Then ask for a yes or no from the editor.

If the editor writes a personal letter in reply, but the editor's letter is negative, keep the channel of communication open by offering another topic, at an early (but appropriate) time.

Should you query by telephone? Many professional writers do, with an outline before them to aid their discussion of the topic. The advantage to telephoning an editor or associate editor are: the telephone call saves the time it takes for a letter to get to a magazine, and a reply to be returned to the writer; the writer and editor may well reach an alternate slant on the story (and thus a go-ahead on the article topic) which might not have been mentioned in a letter; the writer can tape the telephone conversation and use that tape later to jog the memory; the editor and writer may agree on a totally different article topic while on the telephone.

The advantages usually out-weigh the disadvantages. The disadvantages are that a magazine editor may not take a call from a writer unknown to the magazine; or the call may reach the right editor during a hectic period when the editor may not wish to consider new ideas and thus the writer may receive a curt "No"—or the cost of telephoning from the opposite side of the country, writer to editor may be prohibitive (but eventually deductable at tax time as a legitimate business expense).

Do state a probable title and the probable length of the article, at the bottom of the letter. This helps the editor visualize the concept and the size of the article.

Do reveal magazine experience if you have any, including freelancing or staff work even if you were a gofer (go for coffee, go for the mail).

Don't begin with a question. (How would you like an article on topic X?) This makes the query too easy to reject—it's too easy for any editor to say no.

Don't use a typewriter with an odd typeface. Some newer typewriters have typeballs which have faces that can be computer-read. Avoid these and save your reader's eyesight.

Don't hand-write a query letter. Ever.

Don't betray your inexperience: don't reveal you are 'only' a student. Or 'only' a novice article writer. Don't use university stationery. Don't list your return address as a campus dormitory or a sorority or fraternity house. If need be, rent a post office box to give yourself a 'neutral' return address. Many editors don't want to be bothered by students or novices.

THE HARDEST PARTS

Don't fail to ask about rates of payment if you can't determine from reference sources such as *Writer's Market* what the magazine pays. *Always ask:* "How many words for how much?" and "When do you want the piece?" and "I *assume* you pay on acceptance." (If the magazine pays on *acceptance,* when the editors have read the manuscript and have scheduled publication, the writer may be paid relatively quickly. If the writer is paid on *publication,* all sorts of tragedies may befall; the article may be held until the subject is out-of-date; the magazine may change format and then kill the piece; or an editor who originally liked the piece may leave the magazine, thus effectively killing the article. Or it simply may get lost and never found.)

Remember: this is a business deal and you have every right to know what payment is involved and when you will be paid. It's your product, your article which is being sold. You wouldn't do less selling your car . . .

Don't offer an article beyond your own abilities or a deadline you know you can't meet.

If you are writing for a magazine, don't reveal very minor newspaper experience. Many magazine editors believe that their product—the magazine—is stylistically or demographically above the average afternoon newspaper. Thus they want writers above the average newspaper writer. This *is* a stereotyped idea—a cliche—of the relationship between newspapers and magazines, with magazines higher in the pecking order. But while it is a cliche, many editors believe it, even though they wouldn't indicate it in public. It's just one of the small bigotries of publishing (and book publishers believe they are a cut above magazines). Play their own game.

Don't reach too far afield: match the article idea with an appropriate magazine or category of magazines.

Don't entirely rely on the guidelines regarding magazine article ideas, in reference books such as *Writer's Markets.* If a magazine specifies that it is interested in article ideas in categories A, B and C, and you have an article idea that is a very close D topic, query anyway. They may have wanted to broaden their perspective anyway. In any case, all you have wasted is a stamp and some of your time. *Don't entirely rely on* the reference books regarding small or regional magazines. Don't use the reference directories solely. Make sure the magazine is still being published before you write the article or the query letter.

One of the most vexing questions freelancers have is: *should I query more than one magazine at the same time?*

Most professional writers swear by two simple rules: sending material out *on spec* (on a speculation basis—without payment prior to publication) is amateurish; sending out multiple query letters is imprudent. But there is not universal agreement about this, even among editors. In his column,

Do's and Don't's of Writing Query Letters

"Non-Fiction: Postal Mortem," (Nov., 1979, issue) *Writer's Digest* contributing editor Art Skipol observes that he and *W.D.* editor John Brady disagree regarding the multiple submission. Skipol believes that mutliple queries are proper; John Brady believes they are not.

If you *must* write multiple query letters, here's another rule: *never make a photocopy* and add the editor's name above the body of the letter: all multiple letters should be freshly-typed letters. Many secretarial services offer programmable computer-typewriters, into which the body of the letter is stored. The typist types in the editor's name and address. The computer then re-types the body of the letter. That kind of multiple query letter is acceptable, I believe, and the cost of this secretarial service is going down, as the cost of programmable computer-typewriters is going down.

Don't offer more than one article per query letter. This dilutes the importance and significance of the article idea. If you have two ideas suitable for the same magazine, write two query letters at the same time, post-date one by a week or so and mail it later.

Don't offer to make the article significantly shorter (or longer) than the length the magazine desired. If *Writer's Market* tells you that the magazine in question wants 3,000-word articles, don't send one which is half that size or twice as long. The magazine may kill the idea arbitrarily because the size is unworkable for the magazine's format.

Finally, *don't give up.* Many freelancers have periods in which the best-worded and most intriguing query letters fail to generate sales. It happens to all of us. Try again. And again. And again. Re-read the magazine, your article and re-read the query letters to see what you might change, what you might emphasize, how you might re-slant.

On the following pages are examples of query letters which are successful in content and style. Remember: the query letter should be *conversational* and *businesslike;* the query letter should offer *anecdotes* and *examples* from the article and should, if possible, indicate *article length* and *title* and should *ask for a reply from the editor.* The writer should *tell why the article is appropriate for the magazine.*

The following four query letters range from: small, special-interest magazines, (Kelle Banks' query to *Austin* magazine); to medium-sized magazines, (Gale Wiley's query to *Army Times*); to the largest magazines (Hal Higdon's queries to *People* and *Good Housekeeping*).

During her first feature writing class at the University of Texas, Kelle Banks discovered The Corn Popper, a franchise shop in Austin, which sold flavored popcorn. She sent the following query to *Austin,* the Chamber-of-Commerce sponsored city magazine. Instead of a written reply, she got a telephone call. The editors said "We liked your query letter so much, whatever story you've got on the shop, we'll buy it." (Or words to that effect.) *Austin* magazine bought her article *solely* on the basis of the

THE HARDEST PARTS

following query letter. Her article, "Popcorn with Pizazz," was the lead article in the Nov. 1981 issue of *Austin* magazine.

Mr. Hal Susskind
Austin Chamber of Commerce
Box 1967
Austin, TX 78767   19 Sept., 1981

Dear Mr. Susskind,

I have a wonderful story for a future edition of Austin Magazine which I know would be of great interest to your readership.

A new business, The Corn Popper, has opened in Austin and is quickly becoming the hottest thing in candied popcorn since Cracker Jacks. The shop is the first franchise of a business in Dallas. A second franchise could possibly be opening in Austin (the first is doing so well) and another in San Antonio. I predict the store will have locations regionally or even nationally in the near future.

Popcorn is sold wholesale in the store in 20 different flavors—from pizza and jalapeno to coconut and butter-scotch. All the flavors are addictive. It is packaged in white tin cans which are painted upon request by local artists. The cans keep the snack fresh for a guaranteed 60 days ... if the popcorn stays in the can that long. Refills are also available.

The success of the shop is incredible. Even while the store owners, Jan Collins and Sherry McGillicuddy, were setting up prior to its September 14 opening, people came into the store, begging to make early purchases.

The story is tailor-made for your magazine because of the impact which The Corn Popper has already made on Austin business. In fact, the owners have said that many of the bars and lounges in Austin which are buying the snack for their customers are doubling their sales. Also, popcorn is a favorite snack for readers of all ages. As Mrs. Collins said, "It's a one-of-a-kind product for a one-of-a-kind city."

Estimated length for the article is 2,000 words. Black and white photographs are also available with the manuscript. What do you think of the idea? I am anxious to hear from you.

Sincerely,

Kelle Banks

Do's and Don't's of Writing Query Letters

Gale Wiley has spent 11 years as a free-lancer in West Germany. He has written for *The Saturday Evening Post* and *Oui;* and has done background research for "60 Minutes" and *Playboy*. When the Iranian hostages were flown to Germany, following their release, Wiley covered the story from Germany for Mutual Broadcasting, UPI, WFAA in Ft. Worth-Dallas, and a paper in Scotland. Here in a query letter which led to a three-part series for *Army Times* magazine, for a total payment of $1,500.

12 December 1974

Mr. John Greenwald
Army Times Magazine
475 School Street, N.W.
Washington, DC 20024

Dear John;

I have an idea which I think takes precedence over anything else I might do for your publication. I am sure you have read Studs Terkel's *WORKING,* a book about the work that people do. The author simply interviews people about their jobs, what they think of their jobs, and what they think is right or wrong about the work they do. The conversations are simply transcriptions of taped interviews. The technique is straight forward but requires hours of transcription and editing. I am proposing that I do a similar kind of thing for Army Times, but I would interview the entire chain-of-command, from private E-1 to commander-in-chief Michael Davidson. It would be fascinating to listen to these men talk about job satisfaction, what they do, and how they do it. Imagine if a general echoes the comments of a private. It's possible. The working title of the article would be "Working: Down the Chain." I would start with the general and work my way down to the lowest of grunts. Since the interviews would be done entirely in the Seventh Army Command, perhaps a better title would be "Working: Down the Seventh Army's Chain." In any event, I think the idea is excellent. I am interested in how much you would be willing to pay for such a piece. Obviously such an article would require some travel. Could you possibly cover my expenses and pay the regular plus fee for pix? Please let me know and I'll get to work on it.

Gale Wiley

Here are two query letters by Hal Higdon, which led to successful sales, first to *People* magazine and secondly, to *Good Housekeeping*.

THE HARDEST PARTS

March 26, 1981

Richard B. Stolley
Managing Editor:
People Weekly
Time & Life Building
Rockefeller Center
New York City 10020

Dear Dick;

I was on a place last weekend when I came across a column item that shouted "magazine article" at me. And when I tried to think of which magazine, yours seemed like the likely target.

The item was about John and Judith Hilt of Delavan, Illinois, who had just gone on their annual grocery shopping spree, which usually comes when they get their income tax refund. They spent $1654.81 on 18 carts of food at their local supermarket. John estimated that his one-shot shopping saves him $100 on gas and food prices that go up later. (They also shop now and then for perishables.)

I called the Hilts this evening, and he is a machinist for Caterpillar Tractor. He and his wife have five children. They did their first spree about six or seven years ago when Kroger had a special sale on canned goods and before they knew it they had bought $3-400 worth. And it sort of escalated from there.

John lives about seven miles from town thus doesn't want to spend money on gas. They have two freezers now. "The price of groceries never go down," he told me. "When we want something for supper, we just go down in the basement and get it. With five children, we can't afford to eat at McDonald's or Hardy's. We buy stuff that will keep and also get a whole side of beef that lasts three-quarters of a year."

Recently they moved and the owner of the new super-market they went to for their yearly spree thought they were kidding when they first told him their plans. John says: "After we filled the first seven carts, they called the bank to make sure we were for real. Then after 14 carts they called the bank again. At 21 carts, they checked a third time."

They arrive at the market mid-week to avoid crowds and the entire family participates in the buying, loading everything into a pickup truck and one very full station wagon. "Then we work until 1:00 in the morning putting everything away, peas in one section, corn in another," says John.

When they arrived this year, the store manager apparently (warned in advance) did some public relations work and two TV stations and the local newspapers showed up. That suggests to me that this year's spree has been reported for posterity by photographers at the time it happened. And we should be able to take additional photos of the Hilts at home, maybe in that wonderfully overstocked basement, also back at the supermarket if we need to restage anything. I think it's a good picture story and a good people story, or should I say *People* story.

Delavan is right outside of Peoria, and coincidentally my daughter is a student at Bradley University in that city. Mom's Weekend is April 25 and since I will be in the area that would be a good time to do the basic research on the piece. You'll have to tell me whether you would want to send a photographer in then or later.

Regards,

Hal Higdon

March 20, 1981

Jean Libman Block
Articles Editor:
GOOD HOUSEKEEPING
959 Eighth Avenue
New York City 10019

Dear Jean:

I recently have been in touch with Otis R. Bowen, MD, former governor of Indiana, currently a professor in family practice at the University of Indiana. I had met him several times on social occasions. He was governor until this year, but under Indiana law was not permitted to serve more than two years. He is a Republican, if it makes any difference.

I contacted Dr. Bowen because of a recent UPI account of a talk he gave at an American Medical Association leadership conference in Chicago. The headline on the UPI story was: BOWEN GAVE WIFE 'ILLEGAL' DRUGS. His wife Beth recently died of cancer.

The story described Bowen's use of several treatments banned under federal law. He used them to ease his wife's pain. He

THE HARDEST PARTS

obtained DMSO from a veterinarian as well as THC, the active ingredient used in marijuana, plus an unnamed cancer drug from France.

Following the contact, Dr. Bowen wrote me: "I have no regrets about using medicines to give (Beth) relief even though they were considered unorthodox. I did not use, as the papers have stated, illegal medicine. (Beth) had all the accepted therapy and when it was obvious that she was failing in spite of it and still had much pain and needed relief, I used DMSO. It gave her great relief and quick, and without mental fogging. In fact, there was a period of approximately three months when she did not have to use any other pain medicine at all. THC was legally used in an investigative capacity by properly licensed people and it gave her tremendous relief when she took her chemotherapy shots. The other investigative medicine for 'building her bones' was all legitimately used by properly licensed people in an investigative capacity."

True, but Dr. Bowen had access to these medicines because of his status as governor of a large state and also his connections with an important teaching university. Not every cancer victim may necessarily receive such treatment. Also, Dr. Bowen is a strong believer that the federal government over-controls medicine. He believes in less regulation so seems willing to force the issue.

He further stated in his letter to me: "(There is) a need for easy prescription access to these medicines for people that they can help. The medicine should not be allowed for over the counter nor indiscriminate use. I want assurance of safety, but insist that a dying person in great pain should not have to be careful of any long time future side effects. No one can realize the necessity of comfort and relief more than the patient with the problem or the close relatives who suffer along with the patient for weeks and months."

Originally I had approached Dr. Bowen with the suggestion that he might want to do a first-person article, collaborating with me. He apparently does not want to offer his byline, but seems willing to cooperate with a third-person telling of the story. Because of his position as governor and doctor, a unique blending of law and medicine, such an article could have great impact and raise important questions about the right of the dying to proper medical treatment. A possible working title might be: GOVERNOR BOWEN'S AGONIZING CHOICE.

The article approaches an issue that should be of great interest to the readers of *Good Housekeeping*. I hope that you can give me the assignment and welcome me back to the magazine after a too long absence.

Sincerely,

Hal Higdon

Suggested Readings:

Fisher, Jonathan. "Writing Article Queries That Sell." *The Writer,* June, 1971.

Gunther, Max. "Writing the Query Letter." *The Writer,* Sept, 1972.

_____. "Article Research by Mail." *The Writer,* Aug, 1979.

Hallstead, William F. "How to Write a Query Letter." *The Writer,* Aug., 1976.

Henry, Omer. "Nonfiction Salesmanship." *The Writer,* Dec., 1978.

Mueller, William Behr. "How to Pre-Sell an Editor." *The Writer,* Aug., 1978.

Nelson, Roy Paul. *Articles and Features.* Boston; Houghton Mifflin, Inc., 1978.

Pesta, Ben. "Writing the Query Letter." *The Writer,* July, 1975.

Olds, Sally Wendkos. "Write a Query—Get An Assignment." *The Writer,* Aug., 1977.

Rivers, William L. and Smolkin, Shelly. *Free-Lancer and Staff Writer.* Belmont, Calif.: Wadsworth Publishing Co., 3rd ed., 1981.

Spikol, Art. "Non-fiction: Postal Mortem." *Writer's Digest,* November, 1979.

THE HARDEST PARTS

Chapter Eleven

Do's and Don't's of Mailing Manuscripts

The best rules of mailing manuscripts are simply rules of record keeping and common sense. The following topics will keep your free-lancing orderly and minimize loss of material and help your sales by being as professional as possible.

What to mail:

The article. That's obvious. But make sure it is clean. As a matter of psychologically being as professional as possible, I never send out a manuscript with a typescript error on the first page or the first few pages. I try to give an editor material which not only is appropriate to the magazine, but material which is clean. Any typescript errors should be re-typed if possible, erased with "white-out ink" if time does not permit retyping.

A cover letter, explaining that the article is being submitted at the request of the editor (from prior correspondence) or being submitted on a *spec* (speculation) basis. Keep this letter to one page, as a query letter would be, even shorter—to several paragraphs if the article is being submitted at the request of the editor. DO NOT: offer to change the article, lengthen or shorten it, if the style or length may not fit the editor's needs. Any phrasing such as "If this article, as is, is too long, I can shorten it and return it to you." This only makes the material appear less than professionally done. It dilutes the quality of the work. If the article is approximately the length required by the magazine, any offers to change the material make the writer appear amateurish.

Illustrations, photography, other art work. Tape captions on the back of all photographs, identify all individuals in the photos. Tape the caption with scotch tape to the back of the photograph. DO NOT write on the back of a photograph with a felt pen or ball-point pen. These pens will mar the surface of the material and may make the photographs unuseable.

Enclose a 9" x 12" manila envelope, with your own name and address and stamp the envelope with enough postage to cover the return of the material. DO NOT paperclip stamps to the envelope; stamps may—although it is usually unlikely—be stolen by an individual at the magazine and the material will be lost when it is dropped back into the mails without postage. If you don't enclose an envelope and postage, the material may not be returned.

Do's and Don't's of Mailing Manuscripts

DO:

Keep a carbon or Xerox of the article at home. NEVER send an article without making a copy.

Keep a record of what magazine the article was sent to and when. An index card will do fine for this, kept near your typewriter.

Do query the editor if you have not received an answer or had the article returned within about 10 weeks for a monthly magazine, earlier for a weekly magazine.

Do pad the envelope with cardboard if the photographs or other material might be bent or damaged in the mails. Several "shirt cardboards" are adequate for this—usually.

Do use United Parcel Service, Federal Express or 24-hour guaranteed Priority Mail if there is any question of possible damage in transit.

DON'T:

Don't call or write the magazine simply to check if the magazine has received your material.

Don't forget to enclose a return envelope so that the manuscript and material can be returned if need be.

Don't use old mailing envelopes or odd-size packages. New manila envelopes are quite adequate for mailing manuscripts. A little extra cost of new envelopes make the material appear much more professional.

Don't fold manuscripts and mail them in smaller envelopes. Use 9" x 12" envelopes.

Don't staple pages together. Number them and use a paperclip.

Don't staple or paperclip photographs together. Photographs may be damaged by the use of paperclips or staples.

Don't send rare photographs or documents or materials which would be expensive to replace. Query the editor first about use and shipment of rare one-of-a-kind material.

Do not send photographic negatives without first making a duplicate set. If you don't want to have articles lost and make copies of them, you shouldn't want to have negatives lost without first making duplicates.

Chapter Twelve

A few words about style . . . and non-sexist language, use of quotations and quotation marks, statistics, transitions, the deliberate and accidental double entendre, copyediting marks, pros and cons of the literary agent, the physical manuscript and titles . . .

To begin, let's define style as:

*the sum of your past experiences, education and practice; coupled with your
*research and the demands of the topic you have to cover, plus the needs of the
*magazine or magazines you want to sell to and the needs of
*the readers (and their expectations) of that magazine.

Style need be only a simple declarative sentence structure, good grammar, reasonable paragraphing and a logical flow of thought. Or, style can be the artful use of long paragraphs, complicated usage, unusual words and graphic illustrations or examples. As William Zinsser writes, in *On Writing Well:*

> I'll admit that various nonfiction writers like Tom Wolfe and Norman Mailer and Hunter Thompson have built some remarkable houses. But these are writers who spent years learning their craft, and when at last they raised their fanciful turrets and hanging gardens, to the surprise of all of us who never dreamed of such ornamentation, they knew what they were doing. Nobody becomes Tom Wolfe overnight, not even Tom Wolfe.
>
> First, then, learn to hammer in the nails, and if what you build is sturdy and serviceable, take satisfaction in its plain

strength.

But you will be impatient to find a "style"—to embellish the plain words so that readers will recognize you as someone special. You will reach for gaudy similes and tinseled adjectives, as if "style" were something you could buy at a style store and drape onto your words in bright decorator colors... Resist this shopping expedition: there is no style store.

As writer, however, you can analyze your own writing. In *Magazine Article Writing,* Betsy Graham suggests comparing your own work with this checklist:

1. Level of usage. Is the language formal, informal or colloquial?
2. Typical sentence length and type. Are most of the sentences simple, complex, compound, or compound-complex? What is the average length?
3. Sentence structure. Is the word order conventional? Is there a noticeable amount of insubordination? Do such structures as participal or prepositional phrases appear alone or in pairs of triplets?
4. Words. Are most words simple and familiar or unusual and long? Are most concrete or abstract, general or specific?
5. Parts of speech. Is there heavy reliance on adjectives, for example, or do concrete visual nouns and verbs predominate?
6. Figurative language. Is there a presence or absence of metaphor, simile, personification, or symbol?
7. Rhythm. What is the source of rhythm: alliteration, word repetition, or parallelism?

She also writes:

With these elements in mind, examine a passage of your recent writing, noting especially the freshness of your word choices, the shapes of your sentences and paragraphs, and their characteristic rhythm. Do you exaggerate or understate, use long words or short plain ones, prefer figurative language or no-nonsense exposition? Are you wordy or concise? Are your sentences terse and staccato or flowing? Does your prose move with athletic verbs or stand still with forms of the verb *to be?* Is it fat with adjectives or lean in its use of nouns that paint pictures by themselves?

After you have analyzed your own style, compare it with the style of the writers you most admire—especially the passages

THE HARDEST PARTS

that have had a marked effect on you—examining how they elicit response or create an admirable effect.

The keys to eventual mastery of that elusive "style" is: *practice*, writing and re-writing; *reading* what others are writing and more practice. Again and again.

On the matter of non-sexist language: many of us—more of us with each passing month and year, make a concentrated effort to avoid non-sexist language. The male "he..." or the female cliche. Or even the male cliche. In many of the books I recommend to supplement this book, the author uses the now-embarrassing "The writer... *He* shall... *he* will..." Copple, Zinsser, and even the old masters, Strunk and White, in their *The Elements of Style,* refer to the masculine writer without the least admission that there are female writers and authors. In among all the other style points, rules and modes of writing, the aware writer should avoid the masculine—the exclusive—*he* and *his*. A recent book which the writer of the 1980s should have at hand is *The Handbook of Nonsexist Writing, For Writers, Editors and Speakers* by Casey Miller and Kate Swift. Sexist writing now appears quite dated and, more than that, embarrassing. Avoid it as you would avoid the cliche, the hackneyed, the trite. For sexist language does a disservice to us *all*. One and all.

One of the most concise guidelines to the *usage* of quotation marks as punctuation is *The United Press International Stylebook,* a spiral-bound paperback guide often found at the elbows of newspaper reporters and editors. Under quotation marks, *The UPI Stylebook* offers:

> *Quotation marks.* Use quotation marks to set off direct quotation, some titles, nicknames and words used in a special sense. Guidelines:
> 1. Use quotation marks to surround the exact words of a speaker or writer when reported in a story:
> *"I have no intention of staying,"* he replied.
> *"I do not object,"* he said, *"to the tenor of the report."*
> Franklin said, *"A penny saved is a penny earned."*
> A speculator said the practice is *"too conservative for inflationary times."*
> 2. In direct quotations of two or more paragraphs, the quotation marks come before each paragraph and at the end of the last; they do not come at the end of intermediate paragraphs, unless the quoted matter is an incomplete sentence.
> He said, *"I am shocked and horrified by the incident.*
> *"I am so horrified, in fact, that I will ask for the death penalty."*
> But:
> He said he was *"shocked and horrified by the incident."*

"I am so horrified, in fact, that I will ask for the death penalty," he said.

3. In dialogue or conversation, place each person's words, no matter how brief, in a separate paragraph:

"Will you go?"
"Yes."
"When?"
"Thursday."

4. Quotation marks are not required in a question-and-answer format or in full texts or textual excerpts.

5. Use quotation marks for some nicknames and book titles, movie titles, etc. See *composition titles* and *nicknames*.

6. Put quotation marks around words used in a special sense or being introduced to the reader:

The "debate" soon turned into a free-for-all.

Broadcast frequencies are now measured in units called "kilohertz."

Do not use quotation marks around such words after first reference.

7. Do not use quotation marks to emphasize ordinary words. Omit the quotation marks in: *The senator said he would "go home to Michigan" if he lost the election.*

8. When a partial quote is used, do not put quotation marks around words that the speaker could not have used.

Wrong: *The accused man said he "was not in the habit of setting fires."*

What he must have said was: "I am not in the habit of setting fires."

9. For quotes within quotes, alternate between double quotation marks ("or") and single marks ('or'):

She said, "I quote from the letter, 'I agree with Kipling that "the female of species is more deadly than the male," but the phenomenon is not an unchangeable law of nature,' a remark he did not explain."

But note the damage such a complicated structure does to comprehension.

Use three marks together if two quoted elements end at the same time: *She said, "He told me, 'I love you.'"*

10. The period and the comma always go within the quotation marks. The dash, the semicolon, the question mark and the exclamation point go within quotation marks when they apply to the quoted matter only. They go outside when they apply to the whole sentence.

THE HARDEST PARTS

I can't balance my checkbook without my ten-dollar pocket calculator. I am not a mathematician. I am a writer. And professor. I dislike math. I *hate* self-help math guides. I *tolerate* my own calculator and distrust computers. I say that by way of warning: if you have to use statistical material in an article: *beware*. If I have to use any numbers, I remind myself of the acronym KISS, which reminds me to *Keep It Simple, Stupid*.

Many readers have no more mind for math than you do: but you are also the expert who is supposed to make a complicated story clear. Do it: make it clear. Offer statistics in a way which is meaningful, logical, and lucid. Check your math. Recheck your statements. Have a friend re-check your statistical material. Don't assume it is logical. Ever. Check and re-check. Remember: there are many "math buffs" out there who may read your material solely to try and find mistakes in math or statistical reasoning. Or logic. Don't give them the opportunity of a cheap and easy error. If you have one error, they may conclude the rest of the article can not be trusted.

Offer statistical material in ways which the average reader can relate to. Have you ever read statements like "All the dollar bills, printed by the Mint this year, if laid end-to-end, will reach to the Moon and back again twice."? Who can visualize material like this? I can't. Keep the statistics meaningful. Ask an expert to help "translate" formulas and statistics into reality. Could you drown in a river with an "average depth" of one foot? You bet. You might lose your life in such a river if you have a faulty sense of statistics and averages and norms and means and modes and mediums.

Here, by *New York Times* staff member Tom Wicker, is a column he wrote after the death of ex-Beatle John Lennon. Whether or not you agree with Wicker's position on handgun control read through the essay to appreciate the easy and confident way he handles the statistics of murder-by-handgun:

You, me and handguns
by Tom Wicker

New York—On the night of Dec. 8, in New York City, John Lennon was killed by four shots fired from a .38-caliber concealable handgun legally purchased in Hawaii for $169.

That was three nights after Dr. Michael Halberstam was killed in Washington, D.C., by two shots in the chest from a .32-caliber handgun.

Police have charged an apparently mentally disturbed young man with shooting Lennon. A skilled professional thief, interrupted during a burglary of Halberstam's house, has been charged with his shooting.

Lennon was a musician of world renown. Halberstam was well known in Washington medical and literary circles. Thus, their deaths caused much comment in the press.

Except for that, nothing about either murder was unusual. Such violent and unexpected deaths happen all the time. They are almost always caused by handguns, sometimes in the hands of the unstable, sometimes in the hands of the criminal, sometimes in the hands of people like you and me.

Someone is murdered with a handgun in the United States every 50 minutes; it could be you or me, or someone we love, or know. Look at your watch; by 24 hours from the time indicated, 29 persons will have been killed with handguns.

By the end of October, the toll of dead this year from handgun bullets had risen to 6,660. In 1979, handgun fire caused 10,728 American deaths.

This is not a new problem, although the casualties may have increased. During the seven peak years of the war in Vietnam, for example, 40,000 Americans were killed in action; during the same years, 50,000 Americans were killed with handguns in the nation's streets, barrooms, households and public places.

But death is just the most grievous consequence of handgun use. Next year, about 250,000 Americans will be victimized in some way—robbed, raped, injured as well as murdered—by other Americans wielding handguns. That's as if everyone in a city the size of Sacramento, Calif., were to become a handgun victim.

In 1978, in New York City alone, 23,000 robberies were committed at the point of a handgun. Handgun killings in the city totaled 882. Police that year confiscated 9,100 handguns— a useful effort but a minuscule result.

Minuscule, because no one should be in doubt about what causes this record of carnage, violence and crime. The reason is that, for anyone who wants one, too many handguns are too easy to obtain—a fact which no amount of sophistry and self-delusion and gun-lobby propaganda can refute.

When Peter L. Zimroth, the chief assistant district attorney for Manhattan, was asked by Edward A. Gargan of *The New York Times* how two boys who had been arrested had obtained handguns, he made the essential point:

"If you take seriously the estimate that there are one to two million guns in the city, the question is how a kid can't get a gun."

That estimate is to be taken seriously indeed. It may be conservative. Nationally, 55 million handguns are believed to be in circulation. Every year, about 2.5 million more join the

THE HARDEST PARTS

total—nearly 2 million manufactured in this country, several hundred thousand imported. Handgun Control of Washington, D.C., estimates 100 million handguns will be in circulation in the U.S. by the end of the century.

Many of these handguns are easily obtainable through the 175,000 dealers now licensed by the federal government. In many states, notably in the South, no more than a driver's license is required for identification of the buyer, and the license need not even be checked for authenticity.

Other handguns by the thousands are little more difficult to acquire through the illegal traffic that flourishes in every city. Thousands of guns are also stolen every year, obviously not by persons with a legitimate need.

John Lennon and Michael Halberstam are dead primarily because of the easy availability of handguns. So are thousands of other Americans this year, last year, every year. And those statements cannot be refuted by the mere argument that some would still have died if handguns were tightly controlled, or that some would have been killed even if all handguns were confiscated. Of course some would have been; but most who were killed by handguns would be alive if Americans were willing to see these weapons adequately controlled or confiscated.

In the standard-length magazine article, the writer may encounter three or four or as many as ten sub-sections. Trying to tie all these sub-sections (the lead, the distant past, the recent past, personality portraits, quotations, summary material) together involves the use of *transitions*. Most writers don't have much trouble with transitions *inside* the sub-section which may be one or two or three manuscript pages long: the problem lies in bridging the gap between one section to another. Here are some types of transitions which help this jump from sub-topic to sub-topic:

The Spacebreak: This is a physical separation of text on the page. If you are typing double-spaced copy, when you need a spacebreak transition, jump six lines. The "air" or white on the page will indicate to the reader that a different topic is upcoming. Many writers will use a "bullet" a large, heavy dot in the middle of the spacebreak to indicate to editors and printers that the spacebreak is deliberate, not accidental. (The British term for "spacebreak is "line white.")

The Spacebreak-with-filler: This is the spacebreak on the page, with additional material inserted, such as song lyrics, poetry sections, an excerpt from a short story, or perhaps quotations. Use this material with discretion. If you are citing the works of a poet, or writer or lyricist, be sure to get formal "permission" to quote material which may be copyrighted.

A Few Words About Style

Use small amounts so as not to confuse or sidetrack the reader.

The dateline or diary transition: This is a simple time-technique: *"By late 1974,* Joe Smith had gone to Canada and had . . ." This offers a quick and clean transition into an anecdote or other sub-topic within your article.

The argumentative: Let one personality in your article make one statement; let subject B answer A as a way to transition into a sub-section about B. This, from an article about hobos, is an example of such a transition:

> The harangue over, (Hardrock) leaned back.
> "You can just say that ol' Hardrock's a retired prospector."
> "You can just say that Hardrock's a drunk," Jim "Big town" Gorman said, when I met him later on the street. "He and The Pennsylvania Kid are nothing but drunks and panhandlers. I guess that I'm the only true hobo here anymore . . ."

The metaphor transition: Here the writer uses a fanciful style to move smoothly from one sub-topic to another. Here's a metaphor transition in Robert H. Boyle's "The Strange Fish and Stranger Times of Dr. Herbert R. Axelrod":

> "The *Encyclopedia* was a success, and we sell 15,000 copies a year. We've been shooting craps in the publishing business for the last 10 years, and we've been winning." In point of fact, Dr. Axelrod is a very lucky crap shooter. He remembers a night in Haiti when he rolled 17 straight passes, then played 21 and beat the dealer.

Here Robert Boyle uses the metaphor of gambling in publishing (shooting craps) to a literal anecdote about gambling.

In the February, 1981 issue of *Smithsonian* magazine, Donald Schueler profiled Colin Fletcher, author of backpacking classics including *The Thousand-Mile Summer, The Man Who Walked Through Time* and *The Complete Walker.* Schueler interviewed Fletcher during a long hike through the California mountains. In one section of the article, Schueler uses the metaphor of psychologically wrestling (grappling) with Fletcher's ideals, to physically grappling with the mountains:

> The discrepancy between his alternating roles as guardian of the wilderness and chief proselytizer of its charms is not lost on Fletcher; he assures me that "it is a question I want to grapple with in my writing." Which does not prevent him from grappling with it verbally while ascending a very long 60-degree slope that leads even higher into the mountains. "I salve my conscience," he explains in his crisp English voice, "by not writing in terms of specific places anymore. And I do encourage people to behave properly when they're in the wilderness. But you know, I'm not sure my self-defense isn't bogus."

THE HARDEST PARTS

The concluding statement: Here a quotation or statement by the writer effectively draws a section to a close:

    He squinted into the sun, shuffled his feet in the Iowa dust.
    "Am I right on that? Huh?"

Once in a long while, the writer may find a subject which offers a chance to use the pun, considered by some to be high humor and considered by others to be *the pits*. One article in one hundred offers such a chance. Try the pun if you like. I had occasion years ago, to write a profile of a bread truck driver in Muscatine, Iowa, Mike Berlin, who took time off to travel to Chicago and win "The Peterson Classic," a bowling tournament worth $35,000. My lead was:

    Mike Berlin no longer kneads the dough.

My end was:

    He now has his cake and can eat it too.

By playing on the slang for money as dough and phrases such as "have your cake and eat it too," I romped through the article. For my next article, I returned to serious business and didn't subject my readers to the pun. If the writer is not careful, however, an *accidental* pun or *accidental* double-meaning may arise, to the writer's regret.

Your material should go to the magazine pristine: absolutely clean. There are times that, caught under the pressures of a deadline, you'll have to submit material with common copyediting symbols. Or, in a magazine may return a copy of an article to you, proofread and checked. You have to know the common editing symbols and be prepared to use them. Here are the most common. On the left, the usage; in the middle the symbol and, finally the corrected material.

Paragraph Symbol: ¶   or   ⌊   he died in 1957¶   His son, John . . .
                                              he died in 1957.
                                                                     His son, John . . .

Eliminate new paragraph: He died in 1957.⌉
                                                           ⌊His son John . . .
                                             He died in 1957. His son John . . .

Delete extra word: the ~~the~~ pencil   the pencil

Insert space: His son#John   His son John

Unusual name is correct: John |Smythe| John Smythe

Use numbers instead of word: (Fourteen) persons   14 persons

Same for words which are spelled out
but which should be abbreviated:

A Few Words About Style

    She is from Los Angeles, California
    She is from Los Angeles, Calif.

Reverse words: the|men|three   the three men

Add letter: He is from Uah ...   He is from Utah ...

Lower case: He Moved here ...   He moved here ...

Upper case: He is from utah ...   He is from Utah ...

Delete Extra Letter: He is from Utahh ...
                       He is from Utah ...

Add punctuation: He is from Mansfield Ohio
                  He is from Mansfield, Ohio

Delete extra punctuation: He is from Ohio;,
                           He is from Ohio;

End of article: —end—

    The novice writer may be deluded into believing that: *if I only had a literary agent to sell my articles, I could succeed.* This is a snare and a trap. Many—if not all—literary agents will not sell articles for novice writers simply because there is no profit in the occasional sale for the agent. Almost all literary agents work in midtown New York City, where rents are high and thus profits must be high. Agents take a commission of 10 percent (now some are taking 15 percent). To make a decent profit, agents will sell articles to the highest paying magazine ($1,000 and up, through $2,000 and $3,000 ...). Agents are largely interested in selling book manuscripts; with a book manuscript, they may also be able to sell at the same time, paperback rights; serial rights to condense the chapters into newspapers or newspaper syndicates; movie rights; foreign rights in either hardcover editions or paperback editions or both. With these multiple sales programs, the agent can do well for his author and for himself. The single article, sold one at a time, has little potential for the agent. Thus many will not take on articles.

    A literary agent *may* take on a single non-fiction article if there is a possibility of selling the dramatic or screen rights to the article. More and more, this is a common practice. The film "Urban Cowboy," with John Travolta, was originally a non-fiction article in *Esquire;* there are other such article-to-screen examples.

    The agent *may* take on an article if the writer has a book-in-progress, which the agent can later sell on the basis of sample material or the complete manuscript. But if the article writer has no such book in mind or in the typewriter, the agent (and rightly) will not likely be interested in the writer. It's all a mercenary business; the article writer has to be an attractive

THE HARDEST PARTS

potential success for the agent to be interested.

David Lampe suggests that the writer may not be working to maximum advantage if an agent handles the articles, simply because the agent may know little of techniques for secondary sales, the subsequent sale of the article to a foreign magazine, or the sale of the article to non-competing magazines. The agent simply may not be interested in pursuing this Grail. The writer can and should be interested in maximum sales for the completed article: the agent may not care. Additionally, the agent acts, accidentally or deliberately, as a barrier between writer and editor. The writer may wish to negotiate with the editor for additional articles; the agent may not wish to do so.

One word of caution is necessary here: the literary agent is occasionally thought of as the "used car salesman" or the publishing business. Not all are completely ethical. The writer should look for an agent listed in the Society of Authors Representatives (headquartered in New York), which is the trade association of the agency business.

The best autobiography of a literary agent is Paul R. Reynolds' memoir *The Middle Man*.

What should a manuscript look like, which is submitted for publication? The following shows a first page. The writer does *not* submit a magazine article like a college or university paper, with a title page. The first page offers the title.

The second and subsequent pages should contain the headline (or slugline) of the article and the writer's name and the page number, at the top of the page. The writer need not write MORE at the bottom of each page; at the end of the article simply write —end—.

```
Your name                          Copyright data OR
Address                            "Approx. XXXX words"
City, zip code
```

(skip at least 15 lines)

Title here, flush left or centered (flush left easier)
By-line here, flush left or centered

A Few Words About Style

Your copy begins here, at least half-way down the page; leave enough margins at sides, at least one inch or one-and-a-half inches. Leave enough bottom margin—an inch or inch-and-a-half.

The use of (MORE) at the bottom of the page is newspaper style but not magazine style. The top of the second and subsequent pages should contain the title, the author's name and the page number. And so on . . .

 XXXXXXXXXXXXXXXXXXXXXXXXXXXXXXXXXXXXXX
XXXXXXXXXXXXXXXXXXXXXXXXXXXXXXXXXXXXXX
XXXXXXXXXX.

 XXXXXXXXXXXXXXXXXXXXXXXXXXXXXXXXXXXXXX
XXXXXXXXXXXXXXXXXXXXXXXXXXXXXXXXXXXXXX

Do magazines steal ideas? Generally no. If you submit an idea in the form of a query letter or a completed manuscript, and get a "thanks but no thanks" form rejection letter, but see essentially the same story *idea* later in the same magazine, it just may be that the magazine had the same idea in progress and simply neglected to inform you in their reply to your query or article.

The other side of this coin may be the following, from a special advertising supplement "So You Want to be a Free-Lance Writer?" by Ken Scheck, which appeared in *Newsweek* in the spring, 1982 (approx. March 1):

> A free-lance writer, a fellow with several years of experience and a dozen published articles to his credit, mails off a query to a nationally distributed monthly magazine. Weeks later he receives a form letter explaining that his proposed article idea "does not meet the editorial needs" of the publication. However, the editor includes a handwritten note inviting the writer to try again with other story suggestions. A few months later, the writer happens to glance through an issue of the same magazine. There, under the byline of a staff writer, he finds his rejected story idea prominently displayed as the lead feature. Was it theft or mere coincidence? Whatever, the writer submits no further story suggestions to that particular magazine.

Remember, *facts by themselves* or *ideas by themselves* can not be copyrighted; the writer can copyright unique arrangements of facts, approaches, quotations, slants and conclusions. The writer can copyright an entire article including facts, ideas, syntax and conclusions. Especially new conclusions and insights based from previous material.

Fortunately theft of ideas seldom happens. To prevent the possibility of theft, come to new conclusions, using your own interviewing and style, copyright your article and keep a Xerox or carbon.

THE HARDEST PARTS

A few words about titles: some writers begin with a pre-conceived title and simply write that, then begin the article under it. Others don't have a title until the end of the piece. They then read through the material, find an appropriate summary phrase and insert that above the first page material. Either way (I prefer the former technique), the title should summarize the article. In some cases, you can use quotations or paraphrased quotations, or questions. It is preferable, however, to use summary titles for most pieces.

Do *not* rely on editors to supply a title to your article. They have too much to do to supply a title—more importantly, you are the authority for your article and presumably could supply a better title than the editor who buys it for publication. Many titles have an implied verb; the *action* verb is often implied. Titles which have puns should be keyed to magazines which use such titles, many do not. Don't be upset if a magazine changes your title; for space reasons many titles are changed and shortened. If a magazine runs my article without any editorial change, but does change the title for space reasons, I am satisfied. They published what I wrote: the title is a give-or-take thing.

Most good titles are between five and seven words excluding articles *the, and, an, a.* In *The Magazine Writer's Workbook,* John C. Behrens offers these guidelines for writing titles:

> The following is a list of the more popular types of titles used in magazines today.
>
> 1. *STRIKING STATEMENT.* Usually a statement gleaned from the article that can jolt the reader. The difficulty, especially in an era of dramatic overuse of sensationalism in magazine journalism, is avoiding exaggeration or offending good taste. Some examples of striking statements are such titles as "Vassar G-Stringers," story about Vassar College's all-girl singing group, in CAMPUS STREET Magazine; "Air Academy Cheating Scandal" in LOOK Magazine or COSMOPOLITAN's "Mother to 45,000."
> 2. *LABEL.* Such titles set forth the obvious without an attempt to stimulate. There is no obvious attempt to lure readers. For example, "Latin Americans in New York," "Umpire School" or "States Rights."
> 3. *PARAPHRASE OR PUN.* Using a well-known quotation, movie title, song or familiar saying to attract attention. "A Tale of Two Empires," "Rats Bite the Dust," or "Time Marches Back."
> 4. *DECLARATIVE SENTENCE.* A concise sentence with strong subjects and verbs. "Our Schools Are In Danger,"

"The Prank That Changed My Life," "1967—The Year To Stretch Your Dollar," or "Carney Goes On A Second Honeymoon."
5. *HOW, WHY AND WHAT.* Such titles are usually used on stories of advice. They are most often seen in business and trade journals. Some examples are "What To Do Before You Paint," "How Young Mothers Steal Time for Themselves," "How to Pick the New Fall Lines," and "Suicides: How to Spot Danger and What To Do About It."
6. *QUESTION.* Frequently used title device which forces the reader to seek the answer. The writer's most difficult problem is making the question broad enough to encompass the general reader. "Is It Time to Buy Or Sell?" "Who's Making the Big Money?"
7. *DIRECT ADDRESS.* Talking to the reader in first or second person titles such as "You Can Live on $5000 A Year In Puerto Rico," or "You Can Ski If You Want To."
8. *QUOTATION.* Quotations of general nature are sometimes effective as titles. The basic problem for the beginner is making sure the quotes are familiar to the public. "Fire When Ready, Mr. Gridley," "Wait Till You See The Whites Of Their Eyes."
9. *EXCLAMATION.* Though once used extensively, exclamation titles are not vogue today. Readers today are suspicious of shock headlines that add emphasis by using the exclamation point. "I Say It's Double Talk!" "Let the Older Men Alone!" "Don't Strike That Match!"
10. *RHYME AND ALLITERATION.* Though effective if used properly, alliteration has become an overworked device of newspaper as well as magazine editors. Since it can easily become dull or trite, beginning writers should use rhyme and alliteration with care. "Fit For Fishermen," "Confessions of a Clergyman," "Rocks of Good Stock."

Novice writers should keep in mind that *titles don't sell articles.* The writer's title is usually the first item to be changed by a magazine and is usually the least important.

Suggested readings:

Behrens, John C. *The Magazine Writer's Workbook.* Columbus, Ohio: Grid, Inc., 1972. Rev. ed.: Holland Patent, N.Y. Steffen Publishing Co., 1984.

Cleaver, Diane. "All About Agents." *Writer's Digest,* June, 1980.

Graham, Betsy. *Magazine Article Writing: Substance and Style.* New York: Holt, Rinehart & Winston, 1980.

Gunther, Max. "Using Quotes in Nonfiction Writing." *The Writer,* Sept., 1978.

Jacobson, Emilie. "The Literary Agent and the Freelance Writer." *The Writer,* July, 1972.

Miller, Bobby Ray, ed. *United Press International Stylebook.* New York: United Press International, 1977.

Miller, Casey and Swift, Kate. *The Handbook of Nonsexist Writing for Writers, Editors and Speakers.* New York: Lippincott & Crowell, 1980.

Reynolds, Paul R. *The Middle Man.* New York: William Morrow, Inc., 1972.

"Should You Really Have an Agent?" *The Writer,* July, 1971.

Strunk, William and White, E.B. *The Elements of Style.* New York: Macmillan, 3rd ed., 1979.

Weisbord, Marvin, ed. *A Treasury of Tips for Writers.* Cincinnati: Writer's Digest Books, 1965.

Weisinger, Mort. "Titles That Talk." *The Writer,* August, 1975.

Chapter Thirteen

Twelve Ways to End Your Article Gracefully

All good manuscripts must come to an end, and if they come to a good end, they will be even better. Here are a dozen types of conclusions you can use.
             by Robert L. Baker

Reams of copy have been written about leads, story organization and development. You will find very little in our professional literature, however, about closes, possibly the most significant and the most memorable segment of any feature article.

This is both puzzling and unfortunate.

We may be adept at snaring our readers with brilliant graphics, tempting heads, and exciting leads, and we may have the writing talent to keep them enthralled through paragraph after paragraph of body copy. But if there is a let-down at the end, if we fail in fashioning a strong, *memorable* finish, all could be for naught and readers will lay our work aside with a shrug and wonder why they read the piece.

It adds immeasurably to the pleasure of a new musical if you can leave the theater with at least one catchy tune to whistle. It is equally satisfying to finish reading anyone's editorial piece with at least one useful and stimulating idea lodged in your mind. And it is my personal contention that the close is where this mental implantation is most likely to occur—not in the lead, not in the body.

Robert Baker is president of the Chicago-based PR agency, Baker & Bowden. He is also the editor and publisher of the communications newsletter *Impact*, published continuously since 1959. This article first appeared in *Impact*.

THE HARDEST PARTS

What we must understand, particularly in our feature writing, is that we are basically storytellers. A feature article should be more than a drab recitation of facts. It should embody all the characteristics of an essay, a play, a short story. The basic framework is clear and obvious. We start with a theme, an idea, or a news peg. We develop this theme or idea point by point in the body of the story. And then comes the ending, the conclusion, the close.

"Your article must have a theme, make a point of some kind, drive toward a conclusion," author Max Gunther advices. "It must lift the reader up, carry him along, and set him down with a satisfying thump—and he must end with a strong sense of having arrived somewhere, of being in a different place from the place where he started."

If we could convert article-writing theory into a visual form, it might look something like this (we're assuming a feature that builds gradually to a high point or climax):

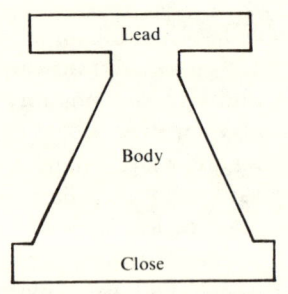

```
    ┌──────────┐
    │   Lead   │
   /└──────────┘\
  /              \
 /      Body      \
 \                /
  \              /
  ┌──────────────┐
  │    Close     │
  └──────────────┘
```

The lead, of course, is the "show window" of any article; a promise of great things to come; a pacesetter and moodsetter for the story and facts that follow; the match that lights the fuse of interest.

We all realize how critical a lead can be. We all know it needs to be clear, concise, provocative, vigorous, and true to the facts that follow. The mood and manner of the lead should predict the mood and manner of the story.

Another fact in writing leads that is seldom considered: A good lead paves the way to a good "close." One "teases" the reader into the story; the other "teases" the point of the story into the reader.

A transitional statement or paragraph carries you out of your lead into the body of the story where you can elaborate as space permits on the lead's promise and develop the storyline through employment of all the various devices of the article writer—anecdotes, quotes, specific examples, lively presentations and verifications of fact and opinion, even dialogue.

The readers, as they read, begin to feel that the story, if it is properly and excitingly written and paced, is building in fascination and merit, that it's leading somewhere to their benefit, driving toward a significant and worthwhile conclusion.

So, finally, we come, we hope, on an upbeat of interest and with great expectations, to that final statement or paragraph, the climax or coda of your work.

Your close should represent some of your keenest thinking and your finest and most carefully prepared prose.

Just as it pays to be constantly "lead sensitive" when you are assembling facts and photographs for a story, so it helps to be "close conscious." Many writers will slug at least one page of their notes "lead" in hopes that inspirational lightning will strike long before they start composing page one. The same procedure should apply for closes. Keep a page of notes slugged "close" and, as your editorial research progresses, jot down thoughts as they come to you.

There are undoubtedly some editors and writers who believe that no connection need exist between an article's lead and its close. Possibly so, but it is my conviction that the lead ought to be written with the close not entirely out of mind. In my many years behind a typewriter, I have relied on three primary sources of inspiration for my closes, in this order: 1) the lead, 2) the story objective, 3) ideas that germinate from body copy, usually body copy in the paragraph or two preceding the closing paragraph.

There are no mechanics, no rules, no magic blueprints to follow when writing your close. If, however, you know the various ways of ending a manuscript, you can select and work with the one that best suits your article. Here then are 12 types of closes I have identified. (Most of the examples that follow were pulled from a single publication—International-Stanley Corporation's *Inside Story*, a magazine for railroaders and grain trade readers.)

The Lead Replay

As the name implies, this is a duplication or a rewrite of the lead, occasionally with some amplification. Or it could be simply a repeat of the lead's theme as in this example from an article on railroad lore.

> Lead
>
> As she flies through Colorado
> She gives an awful squawl
> they tell her by her whistle
> —the Wabash Cannon Ball.

Why, that train went so fast, after it was brought to a dead stop it was still making 65 miles an hour!
Then they speeded up the schedule.

Close

Though the big laughers may have now passed on, on balmy nights when the stars are high in the heavens, if you listen hard, you'll hear a whistle that laughs like a man and keeps the hills echoing with wild laughter as the train races by . . .

The Proximity Close

Tap the material immediately preceding your final paragraph for a closing angle, like this example written by Richard F. Janssen for "The Outlook" column in *The Wall Street Journal:*

Preceding Paragraph

What worries Ralph Bryant of the Brookings Institution, a liberal bastion in Washington, is that inflation will remain high for several years, causing "a period of disillusion" and Reaganite resort to traditional "austerity" policies after all. In relying mainly on expectations, he frets, the administration is relying mainly on "hope."

Close

That hope, at least, is widely shared.

Another example from an article about a grain grower and exporter in the Pacific Northwest:

Preceding Paragraphs

As one grower said, "There is nothing so satisfying as growing food in the Pacific Northwest."
"And," he added, "we do it well."

Close

Behind that simple statement is the reason why North Pacific is now able to embark on its second half-century of moving food from its "little corner of the world" into the bellies of the hungry all over the globe.

The Restatement of Purpose

Every article has a purpose, or it should have. Occasionally, a vivid and colorful restatement of that purpose makes an effective close.

The purpose of the article about the Union Pacific was to show new efficiencies and economies in moving large volumes of grain from the Midwest to the West Coast. Here's how the article closed:

Whether it's "Westward Ho!" for a 75-car grain train, or an

12 Ways to End Your Article

overnight 25-car domestic shuttle, the U.P. has one goal in mind: the movement of far greater quantities of grain as economically as possible and with far greater dispatch and efficiency.

By every statistic, success in meeting this commitment has been achieved.

U.P.'s grain trains have, indeed, turned into "gravy trains" for everyone involved.

And this article, the purpose being to show how important the Federal Grain Inspection Service (FGIS) is to U.S. standing in world grain markets. It closed:

To reach a level of performance and product quality unmatched by any other country supplying grain to the food markets of the world, our nation must do more to develop and preserve absolute integrity in the inspection, weighing, handling and certification of U.S. grain.

And for accomplishing this mission, the FGIS is the best tool at our nation's command.

The Play on Words

You can get too cute, of course, but sometimes alliteration, sloganeering, catchy phrases, etc., make the most vivid impression and stick longest with the reader.

This hobby story for an oil company publication about a budgerigar (an Australian parakeet) that preens for hours in front of a mirror shows both a definite connection between lead and close and a good example of The Play on Words ending.

Lead

Your first indication of something unusual would be a whirr of wings, a streak of blue, a tiny object using your cranium as a landing field, and the sound of those beautiful words:
"I love you!"

The Close

He will stand for hours preening himself and rubbing his beak furiously against the mirror, all the time muttering to himself like a tuned down Donald Duck.

It might not be all vanity. Perhaps it's because the little lovebird has no lovebird to make love to.

Or this profile of ConAgra, an Omaha-based agri-business giant. It closed:

But a famine-threatened world's hunger for food continues to grow. And as the world's need for food grows so grows the need for companies like ConAgra, the uncommon company that handles "common" business so uncommonly well.

The Quote Close

Use a quote taken from a subject, from history, even from a sign on the scene, as in this example from an article about the Minneapolis Grain Exchange.

> "American consumers are willing to pay more for the best," Wilkens says, "and American producers deserve to earn a premium price for a premium product."
>
> At one sample table, some wag had tacked a small sign to the wood that phrased this marketing philosophy on a different plane.
>
> "Quality is like buying oats," the sign reads. "If you want nice, clean, fresh oats, you must pay a fair price. However, if you can be satisfied with oats that have already been through the horse . . . that comes a lot cheaper!"

The Add-On

The close can be used to make a point never made before in the story. Sort of a "saving the best for the last" theory. It could be a "shocker" withheld deliberately until the last editorial moment, or, more commonly, an add that just seemed a natural for making your final point.

This example is from an article about railroading in Alaska. The best in this case, was definitely saved for last.

> Then there is always the dream that someday there will be a land rail connection through the Yukon and British Columbia to the "lower 48."
>
> When that happens—and studies are underway proving that it could—the old "moose gooser" will achieve its ultimate destiny.

The Anecdotal Ending

Using this approach, you can either end with a complete anecdote or use the split-anecdote technique in which you start telling an anecdote early in the article, maybe even in the lead. Halfway through your anecdote you stop. You then carry on with the rest of the article, completing the anecdote in your close. These two examples, one about the nation's first Secretary of Transportation (Alan S. Boyd) and the other about the current president of the Union Pacific Railroad (John C. Kenefick), show the use of the pure anecdote (in humorous form) and a reasonable approximation of the split anecdote. In the latter case, however, the soccer anecdote in body copy was not interrupted but used to wrap up the story.

Boyd's story for the day at a recent transportation confab was about the missionary who went to Africa without the usual survival equipment, relying entirely on faith. Shortly after his arrival in the jungle, the minister encountered a lion. Without a moment's delay he got down on his knees, and the lion sat back on his haunches. After a brief silence, the lion said "I don't know what you're doing, but I'm saying grace."

The story undoubtedly has no application whatsoever to the Department of Transportation.

The profile of John C. Kenefick, a not-too-effective soccer goalie in his school days, closed in this fashion:

But for Kenefick nothing much has changed his thinking since he was tending that soccer goal in high school. His mind then, as the ball went whistling by, must have been on railroading.

And it still is.

The Natural Close

Do as the storyteller does. Let your story end naturally. No sweat. No strain. You've told your story. Stop.

An example of an article about wooden railroad crossties:

Once the treatment is completed, the ties are transported, usually by rail, to their final destination at trackside. They don't remain unused for long. Track crews, outfitted with a rail armada of mechanical equipment, remove old ties that have "done their time" and insert the newcomers for their long tour of duty as an unsung but vital element of support in moving the commerce of a nation.

The Summary Close

The Summary Close, as the designation indicates, attempts to distill highlights of the story, or tie up all the loose ends. It often points back to the lead or comes through as a summarizing quote.

An example from a profile of Farmland Industries, a giant, Kansas City-based, farmer-owned co-op.

Farmland's utter size and power in the marketplace; its dedication to building a better, more economically secure life for farm families, has undoubtedly kept thousands of American farmers "down on the farm" being where they want to be—the Good Lord willing—and doing what they want to do.

The Straight Statement Close

This could also be called the "assessment" or editorial close. It consists

THE HARDEST PARTS

of a few sentences or a final thought about the subject in your own words, often right "out of the blue" without duplicating your previous prose in the article. It is not a summary. It is seldom long-winded. It is generally short and straight to the point *you* want to make about the story.

An example of personal editorializing from an article profiling the Peavey Company of Minneapolis:

> Peavey Company, in maintaining such a philosophy [emphasis on maintaining good relations with "rural people"] may have grown in 104 years to a company of considerable size and complexity, but at heart, it still functions as a small family enterprise at its finest.

Another example from an article on the world food crisis of the mid '70s:

> "People who know where to grab the tiger can make it squeal," is a favorite saying of Dr. John A. Pino of the Rockefeller Foundation.
>
> It is now time for the leaders of the world to grab the terrible tiger of famine by the tail and make it squeal in terror as it retreats forever from the lives of the living.

The Stinger

An unexpected conclusion, or an ending that startles, surprises or shocks the reader, is The Stinger. An example from an article called "18 Ways to Kill Yourself in Traffic":

> Excessive speed, failure to yield the right-of-way and the 16 other "mistakes" pictured on these pages are dangerous driving habits. If you are guilty of any one of them, you're gambling with death.
>
> And it only takes death a split-second to become a winner.

The "Word of Advice" Close

One last admonishment, warning or word of advice—a verbal finger pointed straight at the reader—is a blunt but effective way to get one final, all-important point across, like, "The next time you think about smoking—don't!" for the close of an article on cigarettes and health.

There are undoubtedly other types of closes in addition to the 12 we have covered here. We've heard one writer refer to an "Echo Ending" in which you pick some word or phrase that has been repeated often and prominently and weave it into your close in a meaningful, surprising or clever way.

Closes, whatever the approach you use, rate among the most fascinating, frequently frustrating and exasperating elements of an article. Fascinating because they offer you the few words of greatest potential to inform, persuade or affect your reader. Frustrating and exasperating, not only because they often are the most difficult portion of a story to write, but also because none that you write will every satisfy you.

Chapter Fourteen

The Three R's for Revitalizing Article Sales

Reading. 'Riting. 'Rithmetic? Forget 'em. The freelance writer's R's are Recycle, Rejuvenate and Revamp—and sticking with them could earn you thousands of dollars in multiple sales.
by Larry Holden

About five years ago I developed a system to breathe life into the "dead" articles in my files. A dead article is one that is either (a) out-of-date, (b) previously published, or (c) never published. Since then I've added at least $10,000 per year to my income as a fulltime free-lancer. That's a load of cash I would have missed out on if I hadn't applied the Three R's of selling articles to my six-feet-under manuscripts.

The Three R's stand for Recycle, Revamp and Rejuvenate. But, because of the positive results they bring, they could just as easily stand for the Resurrection of a buried ego, the Rebirth of a bank account, and the Rejoicing of your creditors. To accomplish the most good—which translates into how to pocket the most bucks—all three of the R's must be used.

Recycling dead articles is the most obvious piece in the more-article-sales puzzle. Yet many writers consistently neglect this R. Some even avoid it. It's not uncommon for a writer to write an article, send it out once or twice and then inter the unsold manuscript in some dark file cabinet drawer. That, my friend, is a dead article.

The cornerstone of marketing that I found my successful free-lance business on is: *Keep Everything in Motion.* A manuscript gathering dust in a file cheats everyone. The writer is cheated out of a sale and an editor is cheated out of reviewing that piece for possible use in his publication.

Larry Holden is a Dallas area freelancer who has written for a wide variety of publications. This article first appeared in *Writer's Digest*, January, 1980.

Be Law-Abiding

Not long ago, I received a go-ahead at *Seventeen* to do an article about Ted Trikilis, whose company is responsible for *the* Farrah Fawcett poster (remember the eight-million-seller of Farrah in a clinging red bathing suit?). After I flew to Ohio to interview the gregarious president of one of the largest poster companies in the world, and completed the manuscript, the editors of *Seventeen* decided that perhaps their young-adult readers couldn't relate to this 34-year-old millionare. Undaunted, I decided that the readers of a good inflight magazine could relate to the Horatio Alger-like story of Ted Trikilis. Editor James Morgan at *TWA Ambassador* agreed.

Holden's Law is that every article—or at least every article topic—will eventually find an editorial home. I honestly believe that my interviewing someone and selling the interview only once wastes that person's time—and my time. Likewise, it is also a waste of my talent. I use the fear of failure as a powerful lever to push me forward, rather than as a weight to hold me back.

To properly utilize the recycling technique, set up a pattern of reviewing your files every two months. This circumvents the tendency to let rejected articles remain dormant. Even if an often-rejected piece has slipped into the files and out of your consciousness, this process will uncover it, allowing it to once again become a sale-in-waiting.

Take out each manuscript and study it. If you have never sold the piece, or if you sold first rights only, you're concerned only with: Can I send this to some editor *as it is?* In other words, do you have to change any of the text before you drop it in the mail. If no alterations are needed and the manuscript still looks neat and crisp, pull out your *Writer's Market,* select a magazine, prepare your manuscript envelopes and send the manuscript out right away. If the text is fine as is, but the manuscript looks "shopped around," retype it immediately and get it in the mail.

Peddling the Recycle

I send out two recycled articles or queries based on recyclable articles every day. This system is routine, consistent, sometimes a tad boring—and successful. I am working on a go-ahead for at least one recycled article query virtually all the time, and many of the recycled manuscripts are sold as is.

After *Esquire* nixed a US space program article the editors had given me a go-ahead on, the still-correct text and good manuscript condition allowed me to sell the piece *as is* to *The Elks Magazine.* I got $450 for this recycled as-is article, which was $100 more than *Esquire* would have paid. Remember, a never-sold or first-rights-only manuscript is doing you no good huddling in the files. It must be in motion.

Recycling manuscripts that require no text changes is a snap. But during your bimonthly review of your files, you will come across articles that require one or both of the other R's—Rejuvenate and Revamp.

After recycling all the manuscripts you didn't have to alter, repeat the review procedure and ask yourself: Can the article be rejuvenated? Have there been developments in the subject which, if included in your dormant manuscript, will make the piece once again fresh, alive and commercial?

One of the thickest folders in my article files is one entitled "Earth Resources Technology Satellites." That's because I've sold some 18 different articles about these man-made objects that monitor from space geological, ecological, meteorlogical and a batch of other "ogical" conditions on earth. My first sale on these satellites was to *The Elks Magazine* for $400. Since then, I've peddled articles on the subject to fraternal magazines, tabloids, women's magazines, foreign publications, inflight magazines, children's magazines and semitechnical journals. My total sales for this topic rests at about $6,000. Notice I said "rests," because I have queries out now that could launch sale #19.

The R's, the W's and the H

The prime reason I've sold so many pieces on Earth Resources Technology Satellites is my *consistent* use of the simple technique of renewing. I keep track of what's happening with these satellites by writing to NASA systematically several times a year to request the most current information and artwork. I also clip all newspaper stories and magazine articles on the topic.

An efficient way to rejuvenate any article is to examine each manuscript using journalism's time-tested formula for a good news story: the five W's and lone H. By answering the familiar *who, where, what, when, why* and *how* asked by a good reporter—while studying each of your dead articles—you can update the details of the piece with ease and accuracy. In other words, while reading a dead article, ask yourself if the *who* of the story has changed—or could be changed. If so, insert the correct info into your rough draft. Then ask yourself if the *where* of the article has or can be changed, and so on.

About two years ago, I sold a story to the *National Enquirer* on the mushrooming number of metal-detector-toting beachcombers and on the millions of coins and valuable rings they retrieve each year from inland and coastal beaches. During my research, I gathered a lot of treasure-hunting info related to using detectors in spots other than beaches. When I applied the five W's and H to the previously sold article, I found I could change the *where*. Under the *where* scrutiny, the article could be broadened to produce a more generalized treasure-hunting article, which I sold to *The

Elks Magazine. A few months ago I applied the W's and H to the treasure-hunting manuscript I had sold to *Elks.* After updating the manuscript by changing the *who,* I placed the article with *The American Way.*

Once you've rejuvenated your deceased articles you'll be surprised at how many manuscripts can be sold to new markets with minimal rewriting. So it comes down to this: some subjects never grow old, they just get behind the times. Once an article's events and facts are brought up to date, once they're rejuvenated, the story is a brand new sale waiting to line your pockets with plunder from a publication's coffers.

Beyond the R of rejuvenate is the more imaginative, more specialized R of revamp. This stage of article rebirth involves finding a new angle or new slant for a dead article. It's like the movie executive who came up with a new angle for pushing two already-circulated films, *Earthquake* and *The Towering Inferno.* The executive put the two movies together and then rereleased the duo to theaters as a back-to-back package: "The Shake and Bake Special." That's revamping.

Revamping long-lost articles is easier than most writers believe. Some writers develop a mental block about finding a new direction for an article they've completed, whether it's one they did sell once or one that they wrote but were never able to unload . . . I mean get published. I have a system that makes revamping an article simpler and involves rewriting lost articles with several concepts in mind. These concepts are seasonalization, changing viewpoints, blending, paring, regionalization, specialization and the "what if" factor.

Christmas in June

During the two-month review of your filed manuscripts, examine dead articles with seasonalization in mind. Gear your thinking six months in advance. Articles tied to a particular season never lose their usefulness. Christmas rolls around each and every year, so a Christmas article you wrote and sold (or wrote and didn't sell) becomes salable in a revamped form every year. So, every June dig out every Christmas- or winter-oriented piece that you tucked away in your files. This is practically a rote process; every other month, pull out your dead articles and project their potential marketability six months into the future.

Besides reviewing articles already connected to a specific season, you can also "seasonalize" other articles. I did an article for the *National Enquirer* about a woman who served as a foster mom for 256 children over a 15-year span. It was a heartwarming story of love and devotion. During my interview, I asked the woman if she and some of her "kids" do anything special on Christmas. They do. So I had a natural way to revamp the article using seasonalization. I queried *Family Circle* and received a go-ahead.

Remember, seasonalization doesn't pivot only around a specific holiday.

THE HARDEST PARTS

Consider the other "seasons." Each year as the tornado season nears I pull out every article I've ever written on tornadoes, rejuvenate and revamp the ones that need it, and find new markets for the slightly rewritten pieces. I seasonalized the Ted Trikilis material by producing an article for *Modern People* with the angle that with every new TV season, the "Poster King"—Trikilis—has a fresh batch of poster heroes and heroines.

Changing viewpoints is another revamping technique. After I'd written an article about "What Celebrities Do to Relax" for the tabloid, *Modern People,* I asked myself, "What's the opposite of relaxing? Working, of course." So I queried *Modern People* on "The Jobs Celebrities Had Before Stardom" and eventually sold the piece. That's changing viewpoint by considering reversing the subject or by standing an existing manuscript idea on its head. If you produced an article detailing ten ways to do something, your mind should automatically conjure up the opposite viewpoint: ten ways to avoid or to sabotage the same task.

Two more viewpoint angles are sex and age. If you write an article on a topic for a men's magazine, could that same topic—with appropriate variations, of course—apply to women as well? An article I did for *Oui* on the history of the bed was shelved due to a change in editorial policy. So I withdrew the piece and revamped the male-slanted lead to display a female "hook." The first version was a sexy narrative featuring a good-looking jock who's assisted in selecting a waterbed by an attractive coed in a tight T-shirt. After revamping, the lead focused on an aware, stylish, in-control young woman who chooses a new waterbed—in the company of the handsome waterbed salesman. I sold the revamped article to *Playgirl.*

The same kind of thinking applies to age. To produce only an article for teenagers when the topic could easily be slanted for senior citizens too is a waste of your research. Many topics can apply to virtually all age groups. Don't let a sale to a publication for one age group limit your thinking and, thus, your sales.

A Likely Pare

Blending is another way to revamp. Blending is simply using portions of several already-published (or, at least, already-written) articles to "build" another article. Since the bulk of my article sales evolve from celebrity interviews, I constantly use the blending technique with articles produced from my chats with movie, TV and stage personalities. I recently sold an article to *Talk,* a women's magazine, on psychic experiences of celebrities. A standard question for my personality interviews is, "Do you believe in psychic phenomena?" If the answer if "yes," I follow up by getting the celebrity to describe any personal experiences. So the *Talk* roundup article was contructed by simply blending an array of psychic anecdotes gleaned from celebrity profiles I had already written and/or sold.

The logical revamping method to follow blending is paring; it's merely the opposite technique. If you've written a complete, definitive article on some subject, don't overlook the possibility of slicing out a specific section and selling it as a small, separate article. From the extensive *Playgirl* article on the history of the bed, I pared several short pieces. So far, I've sold pared segments on new dream research to *The Elks Magazine* and on the "Power of Dreams" to *Modern People*.

For the next revamping element, divide the US into sections—mentally or on a map. If you did an article on a national scale, can you "regionalize" it down to a section of the country? Or, if you did an article for a city magazine, can you expand the scope to a regional level? My article on "The Evolution of Jazz" in the nationally-distributed *The Elks Magazine* was easily regionalized for and sold to *Metro*, the inflight publication for a commuter airline that services New Orleans—one of the birthspots of jazz.

A revamping formula that consistently makes big money for me is specialization: finding special-interest markets for article topics. Not long ago I interviewed Fred Oman, who has a unique business: a gallery of Wall Street-oriented nostalgic art and antiques sold as office decorations. When I put my interview with Oman under the magnifying glass of specialization, I came up with queries to a variety of specialized publications: business, hobby, local and regional publications. The editor of the second edition of *Money Making Tips* was the first to purchase one of my Fred Oman articles.

R You Ready?

The final revamping method is perhaps the most important—the "what if" factor. I used this key technique to generate several articles on the joint American-Russian space venture of 1975. In thinking about the orbital link-up of the spacecraft, I let the phrase "what if" roll over in my mind. The result of this brainstorming was: *What if* the Russians agreed to the Apollo-Soyuz mission so they could soak the US of its superior computer technology? That use of the "what if" factor netted me about $2,000 from the tabloids and fraternal publications.

I also applied the "what if" factor to a UFO story I wrote for *Gnostica News*, an alternative publication. One year after I'd sold the article I came across it in my files and reread it. The thrust of the article was the chaos suffered by the residents of a small Texas town when a crush of UFO buffs searched for a crashed spaceship. By letting "what if" go to work in my brain, I queried the tabloid *Modern People*, got a go-ahead and sold an article. The basis for the second piece: If the people reacted so strongly to the throng of UFO onlookers when they first came to town, *what if* the UFO probers came back again.

The potential of the "what if" factor is almost limitless. Applying it to every article now huddled in your lifeless article file will result in extra sales, and extra cash. In fact, it was the "what if" factor that spawned this article. One day, while scanning my dead articles and deciding how I was going to Recycle, Rejuvenate and/or Revamp them, I realized how well the Three R's worked for me. Leaning back into the soft padding of my desk chair, I mused: *What if* I queried *Writer's Digest* and . . .

Suggested Readings:

Baker, Samm Sinclair. "How to Turn Rejects Into Sales." *The Writer,* Feb., 1979.

_____. "Writing Salable Nonfiction." *The Writer,* May, 1972.

Smith, Kay. "From Amateur to Pro in the Article Market." *The Writer,* April, 1970.

Chapter Fifteen

like a stranger in a strange land . . . Selling the Regional Article to the National Magazine

Like those of us who suffer colorblindness and are unable to see certain colors, the article writer, through inattention or lack of curiosity may suffer "geographic blindness." The article writer may not be able to see article topics in the same town or region or state which could and should be sold successfully to a national audience.

Simply stated, we all get used to our surroundings. This can be a deadly weakness for the writer: the inability to see appropriate stories.

Freelance writer David Lampe is a native of Maryland. He moved to England and lived there for some years (and met and married his wife Ann). When he arrived in England, he began noticing stories which English writers hadn't thought to offer to American magazines.

Later, when he and his family moved from England to Texas, he began again. In Austin and the surrounding area, he read the newspapers. He explored. He (and his wife) became fascinated with Texas culture, events, and topics of regional interest. He saw what others either didn't see or ignored as articles.

The key, he has said, lies in the title of the now-famous science fiction novel by Robert Heinlein. Lampe says you must act as if you are *a stranger in a strange land*. The writer need not literally move from nation to nation, as Lampe has done, to become interested in a new culture, new ideas or events. You simply look again at your home area, *as if you have never seen it before*. Does your local Chamber of Commerce publish a magazine or newsletter announcing up-coming regional events? Ask them for a subscription (perhaps if you show polite interest, you can get on their mailing lists free). Does your state have a Tourist Commission or Aency or Tourist Council which promotes the state as a tourist haven? Ask them to add your name to their mailing lists. Does your state publish a state magazine? (*Arizona Highways* and *Texas Highways* come readily to mind. In fact, every month, *Texas Highways* publishes a list as a back-of-the-magazine feature, which cites upcoming festivals, celebrations, rodeos and upcoming events, which is a god-send for Texas freelancers.) If your state has such a magazine, subscribe to it. You can take the expenses off your

123

income tax as a "business expense," and in many states, the cost of such a subscription is negligible. As I write this, the annual cost of *Texas Highways* is about $7, compared to about $35 for an annual subscription to *Sports Illustrated,* for instance.

How many colleges and universities are there, within about 100 miles of your home? Ask their News and Information Service to put you on their mailing lists. You may generate article ideas from their news releases. Ask the Chamber of Commerce in nearby cities to put you on their mailing lists. Read as many major newspapers in your state as you can afford, or as you can find free in your local library.

Attend regional festivals, pageants, fiestas, even if you have attended previously. This time, attend and ask questions: *could this be a national article? Has this event been covered before? What magazine or magazines might be interested? Whom should I talk to regarding this? If the event has been covered previously, how can I up-date the coverage, change the slant or focus, or re-write this?*

There are many such regional festivals which can be covered for a national audience. The Cherry Blossom Festival in Washington, D.C.; tulip time in Holland, Michigan; the Dartmouth Winter Carnival; the annual return of the Swallows to Capistrano, California (and the annual return of the buzzards to Hinckley, Ohio, which is a true, annual festival); chili festivals in Texas; skiing in Aspen; the sternwheeler riverboats on the Mississippi. *Signature,* one of the travel magazines ran an exceptional feature on the corporation which owns the Delta Queen riverboat. The same corporation owns a sister ship and the corporation is run by a woman executive. The article's title: "She Opens with a Pair of Queens . . ." (January, 1978).

The following article, by David Lampe, is an ideal example of the regional article written for a national magazine. Notice how he explains facts, ideas and terms which a national audience might not be expected to know. The article is conversational, interesting; it probably tells Texas residents more than they thought they knew about their friend. And, since the armadillo is found only in Texas, Louisiana, and parts of Florida, this strange creature should be of interest to readers not only throughout the rest of the nation, but elsewhere as well. This article was published in *National Wildlife,* February-March, 1977 issue and the British rights were sold to the English magazine, *Wildlife.* At this writing, Lampe is pursuing sales to a Canadian magazine, as well as possible sales in continental Europe. Since he has sold only "First American Rights," and "First English Rights," he still owns the article regarding publication elsewhere in the world.

Like a Stranger in a Strange Land

"Unloved and Unloving, the Armadillo Blunders On"

by David Lampe

from *National Wildlife,* February-March, 1977

Farmers and gardeners in Texas curse it for uprooting their seedlings. Hunters in the Lone Star state insist that it wantonly plunders eggs from the nests of wild turkeys and quail. And Texas ranchers blame its countless burrows for crippling their livestock. The party in question is the nine-banded armadillo, a nearly deaf, blind and dumb living fossil that for years has endured the kind of calumny and vituperation that Texans normally reserve for pests.

But in this day and age of flaky fads, kinky costumes and perverse pleasures, even the lowly armadillo has a small but enthusiastic coterie of supporters in its adopted state. Most of them, naturally enough, can be found at the University of Texas in Austin, where the armadillo has become something of a fetish. All over the campus, students can be seen flaunting T-shirts emblazoned with armadillos, or driving around with decals showing the armored creatures in their rear windows. Enthuses one Austin entrepreneur: "You can sell just about anything here simply by printing an armadillo's picture on it."

It is hard to envision a more unlikely candidate for commercial exploitation. *Dasypus novemcinctus* resembles Winnie-the-Pooh's friend Piglet, only outfitted in brown-speckled Bakelite. One word probably characterizes the critter better than any other: bizzare. A holdover from the age of the dinosaurs some 75 million years ago, the armadillo looks like a creature from another planet—or a science fiction screenwriter's version of one. About two feet long (including the tail), the armadillo weighs up to 17 pounds. Its greatest asset is its heavy armor. Small animals can't bite through its protective shell, so when the armadillo is attacked, its first reaction is to roll into a tight ball.

Unfortunately, because of the armor's configuration such a feat is virtually impossible. Unlike its three-banded South American cousin, the nine-banded armadillo cannot draw in its head—which appears to be armored but is, in fact, easily crushed. Most animals that attack it, however, usually go for its hairless, unprotected underbelly.

Just about anything with more sense than the armadillo can catch it. And that means just about anything. Blundering through the underbrush with all the subtlety of a small tank, the nearly blind armadillo rarely notices anything downwind of it and is an easy mark for anyone who wants to grab onto it. If it escapes, the armadillo heads for the dirt, burying itself completely in about two minutes. And if caught by the tail while in the act

THE HARDEST PARTS

of burrowing, the animal swells its flanks until its "shell" plates wedge into the earth like a partially opened umbrella.

Why someone would want to catch an armadillo is anyone's guess. Baskets and handbags made from the animal are no longer tasteful, few people eat them anymore and, as a pet, the armadillo leaves much to be desired. The creature can dig its way through thick timber enclosures and even zoos can't contain it. At the San Antonio zoo, nine-banded armadillos so persistently climbed the wire walls of the enclosures and then fell back and broke their tails that zookeepers there—like others in Texas—stopped trying to exhibit them. Instead, they opted for one or two of the less-active South American species. The handful of people who have managed to keep live armadillos as pets admit that they respond neither to commands nor affection. Captive armadillos do not live long, perhaps because in most respects the animal is very much a loner.

About as steady on its feet and as sighted at birth as it ever will be, the pink, newborn armadillo, its shell plates still soft, follows its mother around closely for only two weeks before stumbling off to live out the remainder on its own. Only during mating season does it again seek out companions.

Researchers in at least three different scientific disciplines are currently taking a look at the Texas armadillo. Geneticists are intrigued by the fact that the armadillo's births are always of identical quadruplets, right down to the same number of hairs on each body. Climatologists suspect that fluctuations in its population and range can help measure long-range climactic changes. Medical researchers studying leprosy use it as a "guinea pig."

The armadillo is the only creature besides man that can contract leprosy and, because each animal is always one of an identical foursome, it is especially suited to controlled experiments. Researchers at the U.S. Public Health Service's leprosy center in New Iberia, Louisiana, have managed to keep more than 100 nine-banded armadillos captive for long periods, but so far they have been unable to breed them.

Unlike so many other wild creatures, the armadillo makes no effort whatsoever to escape urbanization or suburbanization. In many parts of Texas, wildlife authorities are regularly called by nervous city homeowners for advice on removing the animals. "We usually suggest that they catch the bothersome armadillos and put them in cardboard boxes," remarks one Austin parks department official, adding: "Long before the armadillos realize they're in containers that they can scratch their way out of, you can drive them out into the country and set them free. The armadillos probably don't even remember where they came from." One sure armadillo repellent is the mothball. The animals have shown a marked avoidance of any soil in which a few of these pungent balls have been placed.

The armadillo seems to have immigrated to the U.S. from Mexico and South America, but it is not clear when the move was made. Audubon recorded seeing the nine-banded armadillo blundering through the Texas undergrowth as early as 1830. And present-day archaeologists digging high in the Panhandle near Lubbock—a region where winters today would wipe out temperature-sensitive armadillos—have uncovered million-year-old remains of the species. These remains are identical to the animal now found as far east as Florida, as far west as New Mexico and as far north as Kansas. Fossils have also been discovered in Maryland and West Virginia.

"There's ample evidence to show that the armadillo is again moving north," points out Texas wildlife biologist Danny Swepston. "Some of the factors that will limit its range are hard soils, drought and cold climates." Lacking any serious predators, the nine-banded armadillo seems continually to be increasing its numbers as well as its range. One Texas survey found as many as 50 creatures living within a 100-acre area.

The nine-banded armadillo ranges throughout most of the southern half of the western hemisphere. The other eight members of the family are exclusively South American. These range from mouse-sized armadillos to five-footers that weight as much as 120 pounds.

Although the armadillo's propensity for wreaking havoc on farmland and bird eggs has been vastly overblown, the creature is not without its share of bad habits.

It does, for example, uproot seedlings but not as widely as some have alleged. This usually happens when the animal is nosing through soft, moist earth in search of the foods it prefers—grubs, insects, wild berries, small lizards and snake eggs. Even the most hostile farmer concedes that the armadillo gobbles up great quantities of scorpions, roaches and tarantulas. It also consumes the fire ant, a particularly vicious pest that seems to have just one enemy—the armadillo.

Does the armadillo eat bird eggs and chicks? A recent inventory in Texas of nearly a thousand armadillo stomachs did reveal some traces of bird embryos. But the traces were found in so few stomachs that the researchers concluded they were devoured inadvertently while the armadillos were in the process of eating fire ants that were themselves attacking chicks and eggs. Some Texas wildlife authorities now believe that the creatures may actually help save hatching eggs from ant depredation.

Undeniably, the conical little burrows that armadillos live in are nuisances, mainly because on the 50 or so acres each animal combs for food, it usually digs about a dozen holes. But this is not done out of a compulsion to pockmark the landscape. Many experts suspect that the armadillo simply can't recall the burrow it finished digging just a little while ago. These uncomplicated, leaf-lined excavations are a greater problem on suburban lawns and golf courses than on ranchland, where they are usually hidden at the base of cactus clumps or saplings—areas where livestock seldom tread.

In defense of the armadillos' digging habits, some conservationists point out that its small burrows are actually beneficial ecologically, offering shelter to other creatures. Some animals, they say, move right in with the resident armadillos, rather than waiting for a vacancy.

Far less philosophical about the critter's burrowing activities are many residents of Florida. There, much to the annoyance of ranchers and homeowners alike the armadillo population is booming and thousands are killed each year as pests.

The most macabre crime of which the armadillo stands is grave robbing. This old and by now debunked superstition stems from the fact that the animal is sometimes seen nosing through the soil over freshly planted coffins. Far from feeding on cadavers, however, the armadillo is only doing what comes naturally—looking for insects in the softest soil it can find.

Interestingly enough, the grave-robbing charge was most often made back in the Depression by people in the Deep South who got through hard times by eating barbequed armadillo. The meat is not easy to prepare but it reportedly tastes rather like high-quality, fatty pork, and it is every bit as nutritious. Back in those days, the armadillo was known to many as the "Hoover pig."

The armadillo's alleged bad habits are much easier to understand than is its propensity for "suicide" on Texas highways. Unquestionably, the automobile is the most dangerous enemy that the armadillo has had to cope with throughout its long history. Venturing onto roadways at dusk to enjoy the last lingering sun rays, dozens of armadillos are run down by cars each day. Many would probably survive such encounters quite easily by standing still, crouching down and letting the machines pass right over them. But armadillos are biologically unable to control the reflexes that cause them to leap several feet straight up when startled. It is as if they choose to leap to their deaths rather than take the easy way out. But then, any animal with so many odd habits is bound to act a little weird in the face of adversity.

The following was pulled out of the original article and used as a separate "sidebar." This material was not used when the article was published in England.

"Hoover Pigs" Are Very Big in Austin

It's not easy to explain the armadillo's tremendous popularity among some young Texans today. Much of it, however, is due largely to efforts of an organization in downtown Austin known as the Armadillo World Headquarters. Since its opening in 1969, the pop music and art center has been the hub of the "youths-for-armadillos" movement in central Texas.

Why armadillos? "Well, in the late 1960s," says Headquarters Director Bob Hetterman, "some of us were able to find similarities in our lifestyles with those of armadillos. It's got to do with the way armadillos have always been misunderstood, abused and mistreated. They're a harmless animal and in most places they don't do any serious destruction."

Whatever the reasons, the armadillo has clearly caught on in parts of Texas, where its portrait graces everything from clothing to sidewalks. Since 1971, thousands of youngsters have attended an annual "International Armadillo Confab and Exposition" in Victoria, a small, southeastern Texas community. Strictly a parody of the more serious festivals that are held in Texas each year, the event had included an armadillo race that proved highly offensive to both the SPCA and many armadillo lovers. As a result, the race will be replaced this year by another event that appears much more natural for the guests of honor. In this contest, competing armadilos will be turned loose in a sand pile, where they will proceed to burrow underground. The first one to disappear from sight will be declared the winner.

"I guess we're all looking for someting different to identify with," Hetterman explains. "Armadillos are fun. People laught at 'em, make jokes about 'em. And the armadillos can't talk back because they have no vocal cords."

Since they also lack the muscles needed to register facial expression, no one will ever know if the armadillos are having the last laugh.

The famous Armadillo World Headquarters was closed for good the end of December, 1980; but the lowly armadillo blunders on . . .

Suggested readings:

Newcomb, Duane. *A Complete Guide to Marketing Magazine Articles.* Cincinnati: Writer's Digest Books, 1975.

Chapter Sixteen

Multiple Sales: You Can Sell Any Article More Than Once
any article . . .

In the chapter "Where article ideas come from," we said *article ideas are everywhere.* That bears repeating: article topics *are* everywhere. And for every good article idea or topic, there are several methods of selling and re-selling the article.

One of the crucial differences between the way amateur article writers think and the way professional writers think is this: the professional mines every vein; the professional publishes one article then asks: *how can this article be re-sold? What avenues can I pursue to re-slant this? Is there a different market for a second sale? How can I use my basic research again?*

For the busy professional, time is money. The professional can't really afford to research one article, write it, edit it, polish and sell it, then file away the research and never use it (or the article again). Tips and techniques learned the hard way by busy professionals earn "X" dollars more—sometimes the same basic article can be used over and over again, in new ways.

Do you doubt that there are article ideas everywhere? You won't after reading this section. *There are freelance article possibilities everywhere.* Several years ago, after David Lampe met Texas A & M professor Dr. Vaughn M. Bryant, Jr., Lampe wrote four related articles about what he learned from Bryant. First, to *Parade* magazine, then to *Science Digest,* then *Marathon World* magazine, then to a magazine in West Germany. For the sake of emphasis and clarity, Lampe's *Science Digest* article is run first, here. Lampe titled it, simply, "The Expert."

> Dr. Vaughn M. Bryant, Jr., jokes about his particular field of scientific expertise: "Some guys out in California working on the same thing called their project 'Secondary Harvest Investigation Technique.' So we countered by calling ours 'Consumption Residue Analysis Project.'"
>
> Bryant also smiles when he tells you about the most unpleasant aspect of his work: "When I first came here to Texas A & M University [where he heads the Department of

Anthropology and is also an Associate Professor of Biology] I told them, 'this job is like working in a latrine.' But I suppose that they thought I was exaggerating, and they wouldn't put in a separate air filtration system. After I cranked up about 86 samples of stuff and they had to evacuate the whole building because they thought something had died in the air conditioning system—then they believed me."

"Stuff" is the euphemism 37-year-old Bryant repeatedly employs to describe what he probably knows more about than anyone else on earth—ancient human dung. Countless specimens—known in scientific circles as "paleofeces" or, more commonly, "coprolites"—have survived the millenia, dried naturally in arid regions or caves. Some Dr. Bryant collects himself; others are sent to him by archaeologists working in many parts of the world. "The secretaries here—they used to open my mail and have it all nicely laid on my desk. But not now. Not with all this stuff rolling in every day."

Coprolites were identified more than 150 years ago, but for years archaeologists continued to toss aside the human ones as of no interest. However, millions of animal ones, deposited on Great Britain when the islands still lay beneath the Atlantic, were mined during the middle of the last century because their rich phosphate content made them an ideal fertilizer.

Only at the start of this century did a few archaeologists begin to study the human coprolites, at first using crude techniques that yielded very little. Finally in 1960 the late Dr. Eric Callen, a plant pathologist at Macdonald College in Montreal, worked out a way not only to reconstitute the coprolites but how to distinguish human from animal (curiously, only that of the coati mundi, a cousin of the raccoon, still manages to fool the experts).

"Callen showed us how to make coprolites thousands of years old appear new," Vaughn Bryant explains. "When we get one of them back to the consistency where it's nice and moist and pliable, then by very carefully pulling the parts apart and washing them very carefully, we're able to recover very delicate plant and animal material which gives us the kind of insights into primitive man's diet that we're looking for, things that most investigators in the past missed.

"Callen worked in this area for nearly ten years before he died. Because I'd worked with him and because nobody else was doing this research, I became heir to his notes and specimens."

THE HARDEST PARTS

The collection at A & M has grown, now numbers well over 6,000 individual items, a few million and a half years old. Unlike reconstitutable samples that date back as far as 20,000 years, these are so fossilized that Bryant can't even be sure whether they're human or animal. Potassium argon dating, however, has established their age.

He has four specimens undisputably from the Neanderthal period, 90,000 or so years old. These can be studied, but they have broken down chemically sufficiently so he can't be sure if they are animal or, possibly, the products of human digestive systems different from modern man's.

"The main purpose of the collection," Bryant explains, "is to determine scientifically just what prehistoric people ate, whether or not they suffered malnutrition, what parasites and viruses beset them.

"In some cases I'm beginning to think they enjoyed a much better diet than we do, and they were probably a lot healthier than us."

His study of coprolites is enabling him to rewrite as well as to add to the history of early mankind. "For example, everybody thought maize was introduced into South America in about 500 B.C. But we've firm evidence that it was there at least two thousand years earlier."

To determine such a thing Bryant needs much knowledge. "I started with a master's in archaeology, but I soon realized that this and anthropology alone weren't enough. So I got a Ph. D. in biology to become an expert in morphology (the study of plant and animal forms.) You have to know feathers, fish scales, reptile scales, mammal and reptilian bones, amphibian bones. Then in the area of botany you have to understand pollen, plant chemicals, leaf morphology, wood identification. Then—parasitology, biochemistry, and it goes on and on."

Partly because our ancestors ate the kinds of things not always easily digestible, partly because even those that they did digest can still be identified relatively easily, coprolites tell us much more than skeletons or artifacts. "Coprolites," Dr. Bryant says, "give a general indication of a person's health, and they also tell us a lot about the history of diseases. In coprolites we've found, for example, prehistoric parasites older even than those in Egyptian mummies. So far we haven't found traces of internal bleeding which would give us samples of blood for typing, but probably someday we will.

"I once heard a very learned pathologist state at a conference

Multiple Sales

that pinworms were introduced into the New World by Europeans—by fifteenth—and sixteenth-century explorers, Spanish, French or British. But pinworm infestation, very noticeable in coprolites, turns up in New World ones 11,000 years old.

"We've found evidence of other worm infestation, too. Nematodes, amoebic dysentery, that sort of thing."

Coprolites not only reveal what ancient people ate but exactly how they prepared their food. "We can tell if they ground or powdered their seeds. We can tell not only what they cooked but whether they char broiled or roasted it. Because cooking methods change the chemistry of foods. We even know how well they cleaned their food—from some of the fragments of hair and extraneous plant material we find.

"Working out the nutritional value of the food those ancient people ate can present problems. The U.S. Department of Agriculture publishes information on the nutritional value of, say Wheaties or Kellogs Corn Flakes. Or of loaves of bread or anything else you buy in a store, but where do you find out about the nutrients in various kinds of yucca, agaves, hackberry seeds, wild persimmons, cactus flowers, cactus fruit, other things that we don't eat today—but things that coprolites reveal that primitive man did?

"Coprolites have revealed that those people nibbled all day at whatever they encountered that appeared edible. Most often they ate small animals—things like birds, snakes, lizards, mice and other rodents. But not usually the speedier animals that they couldn't as easily catch, like rabbits. And only rarely did they seem to catch anything as large as a deer. They ate tree bark, flowers, anything."

Dr. Bryant and his students for several years have concentrated their research on an archaeological site near the Texas border city of Del Rio. "What we're going to end up with there—and we hope to publish a book in 1980 or '81—will be the most comprehensive diet and nutritional history ever assembled of a single group of ancient people."

One curious spinoff of the coprolite research has been Vaughn Bryant's own personal prehistoric diet. "We'd finished doing some analyses of the kinds of things a group of people who had lived 6,000 years ago had eaten, primarily considering carbohydrates versus proteins versus sugars and fat and stuff like that, and I decided, just out of curiosity, to try their diet on myself.

THE HARDEST PARTS

"Oh, I didn't go out and shop for lizards or the mice or the flowers, but I did go for suitable substitutes that you can purchase in any grocery store.

"Basically the diet was fairly low in fats. Only in recent times, with all our processing and industrialization, have we gone mainly to things that are very oily and very fatty. Butters, cooking oils and so on. The ancients also seemed rarely to eat anything that had simple carbohydrates in them; their carbohydrates were complex ones. Simple carbohydrates—like, say, the processed sugar you put in your coffee—are synthesized very rapidly by the body and immediately converted into sugar and thrown into the blood stream to burn up very quickly. That or be converted into fat.

"But compound carbohydrates, found primarily in many vegetables and things like seeds and certain types of fruit and roots—mainly what these primitive people ate—have much longer chains of molecules and the body takes longer to break them down. It then dumps into the blood stream slowly. Compound carbodydrates therefore not only give you the satisfaction of feeling full, and provide a continuing source of energy, but are less likely to convert into excess poundage.

"On my caveman diet I stopped not only eating things that were high in fats but also the simple sugars. Much of the meat we eat today is marbled, so I tried to go for more things like fish, which are lower in fat content. Also for really lean meat and things like that.

"How did the diet work out? Well, I lost twenty-five pounds in four months, taking me down to the weight I was when I entered college as a freshman. And I still stick to this diet fairly closely. The occasional slice of pie or other indulgence doesn't really matter.

"My wife and kids follow the diet, and it makes them feel better, too. A lot of friends who tried it didn't lose any weight the first week, and they gave up. But if you persist, it works, and the weeks you suddenly lose four or five pounds you really feel great."

Dr. Bryant's research has revealed some very unusual nutrient sources that primitive people tapped. "Long before citrus fruits reached the New World native Americans got all the ascorbic acid they needed—from agave. So we tried it. We roasted the whole plants the way our research suggests those ancient people did. It didn't taste too good, but it was edible, and it was loaded with vitamin C. More of it, in fact, in a single leaf than in several oranges. And our research indicates that the Indians ate agave in great quantities for 9,000 years. They also ate a lot of flowers—which gave them lots of the B-complex vitamins, all in fact except B-12.

"They didn't drink milk—except, of course, their mother's when they were infants—and yet they got plenty of calcium. Their coprolites reveal that they got it from hackberry seeds. In fact, the center part of these seeds is 65% pure calcium.

"And they got calcium oxalate, the same mineral we get from plants like spinach, from cactus—which in fact has an extraordinarily high concentration of it. Too much of this chemical in your body can cause gallstones and kidney stones, but we have no way of knowing whether or not our primitive people suffered these build-ups because this is something that doesn't show in the coprolites.

"One thing we can be pretty sure of is that these people couldn't have known anything about vitamins. We can only guess that they had certain cravings that they couldn't explain, but they knew from experience were satisfied by eating these things that to us—and maybe even to them—seem unpalatable.

"I keep being amazed at what you learn from all this old stuff."

Not all the "stuff" that Dr. Bryant analyzes is ancient. Recently he attended the first international scientific symposium on "Big Foot," or "Sasquatch," at the University of British Columbia, to read a paper on samples of alleged Big Foot feces sent to him for analysis. "A lot of people are hostile to the whole idea of such creatures existing at all, an attitude that seems to me altogether unscientific. I see it as my duty as a scientist to keep an open mind.

"Maybe all the supposed thousand or more sightings reported over the last century or so mean nothing. Maybe the photographic evidence is suspect—although some Russian scientists who've analyzed it say it isn't. Or maybe there's something there. I remember that the last five members of a prehistoric tribe of American Indians, supposedly extinct, for a generation lived unnoticed on a mere five acres right spang in the heart of a vast California subdivision. One by one they died, and then in the mid-thirties the very last of them stepped out of the woods. A lone survivor of the Stone Age, unnoticed for years right there in the heart of suburbia.

"Now if that could happen in a densely inhabited subdivision, surely in the vastness of the Pacific Northwest or on

THE HARDEST PARTS

some of the other places where Sasquatch or Big Foot has been reported there could conceivably be such a creature."

What may—or may not—be firm evidence are the samples of Big Foot feces sent to Dr. Bryant from the Northwest and from Florida. What does he make of them? "Well, the Florida ones are almost certainly raccoon. And the Pacific ones? They aren't from any large mammal found in the area where they were found. They aren't cougar, bear, moose, elk, deer, sheep, horse—or human. From their content they could have been left by a cow or buffalo—and yet . . ."

There *are* article possibilities everywhere. Everywhere. Lampe correctly points out that after the opening lead anecdote about Dr. Bryant, there is actually another lead; the material at the beginning of the fourth paragraph; "Coprolites were identified more than 150 years ago . . ." There are actually three separate and disparate themes in this article: Dr. Bryant; the coprolites and the research into what they held; and the "caveman diet" which Dr. Bryant successfully follows.

Here's the headline and first three paragraphs from *Parade* magazine, Sunday, September 10, 1978:

The Caveman's Diet for a Healthier You

If you eat like a prehistoric American cavedweller, you will be healthier. You will shed unwanted pounds. And you will feel—and look—younger.

Cactus pads and hackberry seeds don't appeal to you? Grasshoppers, lizards, mice and snakes sound unpalatable?

No matter. Although cave people 10,000 years ago thrived on all these things, your own 20th-century caveman diet can consist entirely of normal, wholesome foods—from the supermarket.

The man who demonstrated this is Vaughn M. Bryant Jr., Associate Professor in the Anthropology Department at Texas A & M University. Convinced that cavemen's eating habits were better than ours are today, he put himself on a caveman's diet to prove it.

That's the caveman diet article. What about the "prehistory" part of Lampe's orginal article, "The Expert"? Here's the No. Four, 1978 issue of *Marathon World*, a quarterly "think" magazine published by Marathon Oil Corporation. Here is the headline, sub-head and first three paragraphs:

Indestructible Dust

Microscopic specks of spores and pollen help

Multiple Sales

palynologists explore the near and ancient past.

A little over sixty years ago, a Swedish geologist named Lennart von Post slid his spade into a peat bog in central Sweden. It was the first, elementary but essential act in an endeavor that would win him, finally, a distinction that few human beings can ever attain—father of a new science.

It's a science that today is applied by petroleum geologists in the quest for oil and natural gas reserves. It also tells anthropologists what certain North American cavemen ate—and *how* they prepared their food. It suggests that Neanderthals were compassionate people. It sometimes provides police with dramatic, offbeat, irrefutable evidence. It routinely helps medical researchers track down allergens, climactic researchers to make broad assertions about prehistoric climates, the U.S. Food and Drug Administration to weigh the veracity of certain beekeepers.

The science is palynology—in plainer English, "pollen analysis." Yes, pollen, the very same microscopic grains that cause respiratory suffering to millions of people every year.

Eventually, four successful quality articles from David Lampe's original research with Dr. Vaughn M. Bryant.

Considerable success from literally a lot of crap.

Now do you believe there are article topics and ideas everywhere? Which can be sold and sold again and again?

A skeptical reader might say *but Lampe's been a successful freelancer for almost 30 years and his techniques lead to obviously sophisticated articles. What about those with less experience?*

This is a valid idea—but the techniques are the same.

Here are simpler articles which led to sales and re-sales.

My first magazine article as a free-lancer came about when I was beginning graduate school at The University of Iowa. I read the school newspaper, *The Daily Iowan,* and learned that a national collegiate billiards tournament would be held on such-and-such dates at Iowa Memorial Union. I wrote to several small magazines asking if they would be interested in magazine free-lance coverage of this tournament. *Bowlers Journal* magazine, a Chicago-based trade magazine for the bowling and billiards industry wrote and said they'd like to see XXX words on the tournament.

My first article, "An A+ for the Collegians," appeared in *Bowlers Journal* in June, 1967. Flushed with small success, I wrote to the editors again and asked if they'd like a feature on Gail Allums, the University of Iowa co-ed who won the women's division. They would. My second article "Iowa's Distaff Double Threat" appeared in *Bowlers Journal* in October,

THE HARDEST PARTS

1967. I wrote again after *B.J.* had taken the Allums article and asked them if they would like a feature on the man who ran the tournament, and who, I had discovered, ran bowling and billiards tournaments successfully nationally. They'd heard of him, *B.J.*'s editor replied, try us again.

My article "Bob Froeschle: Master Matchmaker" appeared in *Bowlers Journal* in November, 1967. Were there other markets for articles about these people? Gail Allums was a black co-ed from Chicago. Would a black oriented magazine be interested in her as a national black champion? *Sepia* magazine ran my profile "Lady Pool Champ" in September, 1968. *The Iowa Alumni Review* magazine ran an additional article on Bob Froeschle "Hustler's Helper" in February, 1968.

My knowledge of pocket billiards at the collegiate level eventually led to another article "Action in the Union": Billiards in the Big Ten," in the February, 1968 issue of a now-defunct magazine *Big Ten,* distributed on the Big Ten university campuses. And an assignment to cover the collegiate billiards tournament for *Bowlers Journal* the next year.

Sum total: the tournament, two articles; Gail Allums, two articles; Bob Froeschle, two articles. Billards in the student union: one article. From the original collegiate tournament.

There are almost infinite ways to sell and re-sell material. Here are the three most important:

1). Re-sell the orginal article. Here the article writer has to understand "rights." Most magazines buy "First Rights," that is, the legal right to print the article *the first time,* at the convenience of the magazine. Most article writers are interested in selling "rights" separately. Many magazines, however, buy "all rights," which means they own the article *forever.* The article writer who has sold only "First North American Serial rights" has the opportunity to sell the article again, as a "second rights" article, meaning the second magazine buys the article under the stipulation they know the article has been published previously. Thus the article can be sold again. "First" and "second rights" sales can usually be made successfully when the magazines are *non-competing.* What are competing and non-competing magazines? *Playboy* and *Penthouse* compete for the same men's magazine audience. *Cavalier, Gent, Nugget, Swank, Gallery, Oui,* and others also compete for the same men's magazine audience. Clearly, readers of the *Baptist Leader* would be unlikely to read *Catholic Life* and readers of *Catholic Life* would be unlikely to be avid subscribers to *The National Jewish Monthly.* These are non-competitive markets. Editors of each of these magazines would not be upset if a free-lancer had an article which conceivably would be acceptable to all and

Multiple Sales

submitted to all. Readers of one magazine would not likely see the article in any of these other magazines.

(The story is perhaps apocryphal—but it is said that one person sold the same article over 300 times—the article was titled "No One Votes Where I Live," and it was a moralistic article. The article was sold without changes to every church-related magazine being published. "No One Votes Where I Live"—was a prison and the article writer was a prisoner!)

2). David Lampe's four *crap* articles show an additional technique: write for different markets. To do that, on a common theme, the article writer has to:

*Use a different headline;
*Use a different lead and a generally different theme;
*Use a different length.

Re-read his articles "The Expert," and the leads for "Caveman's Diet," and "Indestructible Dust." Each is considered legally and ethically a different article because each *is* different. Built on different perspectives, using different themes, different quotations and different emphasis. The article writer does not need to worry about "first rights" and other rights, or conflict of interest, if each article is separate in slant, length, use of quotations and anecdotes and market.

3). Build a chain of articles based on a common theme. My first successful sales, to smaller trade magazines and regional magazines illustrate this. Two articles on co-ed Gail Allums, to different markets, yet based on essentially the same interviews; one article on a collegiate tournament in news format led to a second article the next year; one article on tournament director Bob Froeschle led to a second article about him; and so on. If Froeschle had been an Elk, or a member of the Kiwanis, or an Eagle or an Odd Fellow, or a member of any other national group, I might have had an additional sale, a profile about him to a national organization would also have been an appropriate idea.

One men's magazine article I did several years ago, about an Austin, Texas-based country band, "The Cooder Brown Band" (*Cavalier*, Feb., 1979) is an example of this chain-building method. During the research for that article, I did a long, long interview with Buster Doss, the manager of that band. I found him so fascinating I later did an up-date interview and sold a profile of him "The Life and Times of Colonel Redneck," to the now-defunct regional men's magazine, *Texas Girl*. Buster Doss and I became (and remain) close friends. Subsequently, he became the P.R. director for Willie Nelson's annual 4th of July picnic, for 1979. I called him before the planned picnic and asked him for two press tickets; he knew my "track record" in publishing articles was good and I got the tickets. I attended the Willie Nelson Picnic and wrote a piece "Surviving Willie Nelson's Picnic."

> Thus I got three solid articles from the first interviews: the Cooder Brown article; a separate article on Buster Doss and the Willie Nelson article. The lesson here is: *maintain your contacts; nurture your sources; build a chain of articles—if possible—from the same sources.*

Here's the ultimate end link in the chain: the following is a magazine article which I published in *Writer's Digest* in December, 1969 . . .

Turning Magazine Articles into Books

Just as the television executive uses one segment of a proposed series as a "pilot," so can the magazine writer use one article or a series of articles as a basis for a non-fiction book. The executive uses the pilot not only to test the merits of the program; he also uses it to sell the series to prospective advertisers.

Article writers can use their material in the same manner: the single article or articles can be used to sell the book project to a publisher.

There are several ways this can be done. I'll illustrate: Some time ago, after checking with *Writer's Market,* I began writing profiles of billiard players for a trade magazine titled *National Bowlers Journal and Billiard Revue.* After I had done more than a dozen and one-half of these pieces (and illustrated them with my own photographs), it occurred to me that there might be possibilities for a book about pool players. I went back over my articles and discovered that quite by accident, the articles were roughly divided in half; half were about hustlers, men who made their living playing pool. The other half were about tournament winners who didn't gamble, college players and others, for whom pool was a hobby. I had the material, I had the photographs (or at least the negatives) and I had permission from *Bowlers Journal* to re-use the material. I had, for all practical purposes, a book in my hands. How would I finish it? First, to give cohesiveness to the material, I established the profiles relating to gamblers and those pertaining to non-gamblers. In the language of pool, gamblers are sometimes called *lions.* Non-gamblers, amateurs, or the gamblers' victims are sometimes called *lambs.* There was the title: *The Lions and the Lambs.* I added additional articles, comment about pool in general, more photographs; but I had essentially completed this book by the time I had done the series of magazine articles. *The Lions and the Lambs* was sold successfully to the A.S. Barnes Co., the second time I put it in the mail.

(It was released in the winter of 1970.)

Multiple Sales

You can do the same thing, if you have done a series of articles on the same subject.

My other books were also done in a similar fashion.

Sometime after completion of *The Lions and the Lambs,* I did two articles on film on university campuses for *Cavalier.* (See "Tapping the University Community Market," *Writer's Digest,* March, 1969, for more about college-oriented articles.) These articles were part of a series that *Cavalier* was running in 1968 about student film. *Cavalier* had printed articles about the University of California, the University of Texas and the University of Minnesota. I contributed articles about the University of Iowa and the University of Michigan. Knowing that the Barnes people did film books, I sent tearsheets of my two articles to the president of the Barnes Co., with a letter: "You don't have a book about film-making on campus, nor does any other company. There is an enormous amount of material on student film work—I enclose two articles. I would like to do a book using these as prospective chapters. Are you interested?"

His return letter, which I received soon after, stated: "I like your idea very much and I certainly would encourage you to go ahead. I am sending herewith our contract in duplicate . . ."

My third book was based not on a series of articles, but on one article and I used it differently. For a now-defunct magazine titled *Big Ten,* I did an article "Lewis Carroll—The First Acidhead," satirically suggesting that Carroll's classic *Alice in Wonderland* might contain passages that are comparable to the hippie world of psychedelic drugs. The article "worked" in magazine format: it was lively, I think humorous, and it was awarded third place for journalism in the 1969 College Creative Awards contest and published in *Story: The Yearbook of Discovery, 1969.* When I originally wrote the article, I read through all the material that I could find on Lewis Carroll and read all the critical material available on *Alice in Wonderland.* With my published article in front of me, I could then go back and construct a book outline, noting the phrases and sections in which I would satirize Carroll or tie-in my views of psychedelic drugs.

The book was fun to do; it is in large part light-hearted satire on college students and hippies and it is, in part, a satire on academic scholarship. Based on "Lewis Carroll—The First Acidhead," I completed *Alice in Acidland,* sub-titled "Was *Alice in Wonderland* a harmless fable for children? Not on your life, it's tune in, turn on, drop out, baby." (*Alice* was published by the A.S. Barnes Co. in the winter of 1970.)

So the magazine writer need not be limited to writing articles which are all too soon forgotten; using some intelligence and foresight, the writer can and should turn those articles into book material. It can be done.

Suggested readings:

Appelbaum, Judith and Evans, Nancy. *How to Get Happily Published.* New York: Harper & Row, 1978.

Balkin, Richard. *A Writer's Guide to Book Publishing.* New York: Hawthorn Books, Inc., 1977.

Daigh, Ralph. *Maybe You Should Write a Book.* Englewood Cliffs, N.J.: Prentice-Hall, Inc., 1977.

Duncan, Lois. "How to Write Your Way Through College." *The Writer,* Feb., 1976.

Fensch, Thomas. "Magazine Articles To Non-Fiction Books." *Writer's Digest,* Dec., 1969.

——————. "Tapping the University Community Market." *Writer's Digest,* Mar., 1969.

Swanson, Marshall. "Covering the Campuses." *Writer's Digest,* May, 1979.

Chapter Seventeen

Writing the Science Article

One of the most fascinating and potentially worthwhile trends in magazine publishing in the late 1970s and the early 1980s has been the emergence of a whole new genre of magazines: the science fact magazines. *Penthouse* began publishing *Omni*, a slick and impressive magazine of science fiction and science fact; Time Inc. has begun publishing *Discover; Science Digest* has expanded to a regular (9" x 12") format from a pocket-sized magazine of a few years ago and there are others.

As exciting as this trend is, the science fact magazines may offer substantial problems. For many, the science fact magazines are very difficult to break into: the combination of scientific terms, availability of experts who will consent to be interviewed and the problems of "explaining" scientific data and science procedures into popular terms are difficult stumbling blocks.

In their "Guide to Writing a *Popular Science* Article," the editors of *Popular Science* admit:

> *Popular Science* wants and needs good articles from freelance writers. Unfortunately, some of the articles we get are either totally unsuitable or need a great deal of rewriting and editing before they are usable. Many problems grow out of the fact that some writers have misconceptions about what kind of articles *Popular Science* wants. Others arise when the writer overlooks basic principles of good magazine writing.
>
> We have strong feelings about what we want articles to do, the ingredients they should contain, and how these ingredients should be put together. There are many techniques that can be learned and consciously applied to make an article clear, lively, readable, and informative—even exciting and entertaining. This is an attempt to review these elements and explain our approach so that you will know exactly what we're looking for.
>
> It all begins with the reader. You can't do a good job unless you know who you're writing for. The *Popular Science* reader is an active, curious, educated person. He is very likely to be in a technical occupation. He may be a scientist, an engineer, a technician. But whether he has a technical job or not, he is intensely curious about the things around him. He wants to

understand them and how they work. He is also a consumer, and is interested in products. He wants to know both how to judge them for his own use and how they work. So if we tell him how to tune his car, we must tell him not only which way to turn the screw, but what that does and why it has an effect on engine operation.

To meet the needs of this curious, technically oriented reader, *Popular Science* publishes articles in three general categories.

* The first category is made up of articles about new developments in science and technology. These articles deal with many different subject areas in engineering and the physical sciences—areas such as astronomy, physics, chemistry, transportation, energy, and recreation. (We *never* do articles in the biological or life sciences.)

* The second category of articles is addressed to the reader in his role as consumer. They tell him something about a product or class of products that will help him decide what he needs and how to wade through the welter of advertising claims and sales pitches when he gets into the store.

* The third category is concerned with things the reader can do: Tune his car engine, improve his home, enjoy his leisure.

Not everything that follows will apply equally in every case. The whole section about research, for example, has little relevance if you're doing an article on how you veneered a cabinet. But the general principles do apply throughout.

Style, format, and content

A properly done *Popular Science* article is intensely journalistic. Occasionally a writer makes the mistake of assuming that since we deal with technical subjects, we publish articles similar to those in technical and trade journals. *We do not.* Our articles are journalism; they exist to inform the reader and thus must present material in a clear, logical way so that it is easily accessible. *But they must also do it in such an interesting way that the reader is drawn into the story and feels compelled to keep reading.*

Think about it from this point of view. When you as a writer go out to see someone working on a project or doing research, you will find that he is usually very excited about what he is doing and interested in telling you about it. Generally, you will become intrigued, fascinated, and excited yourself. It's your job to convey that sense of excitement to the reader. You must report not only the basic information about the project and what has been accomplished, but someting of the sense of excitement that you experienced as well. Your job is to take the reader on a vicarious trip with you and let him see and feel and touch and smell the things you did. Remember, the reader may never have been in a laboratory, or at least not the one you are visiting. It's a new and different world for him, and he should experience it the way you did. *Show* him, do not *tell* him, what you saw. Do not explain what is going on. Describe it. Use narrative to report what happened. If, for example, there was an interesting demonstration, tell about it in narrative form with plenty of description and quotes. Give him a word picture. Remember, you are taking the reader on a journey with you. Use first-person reaction freely. Record what you did, what you saw, and your reaction to it. That helps make it come alive for the reader.

Do not, for example, say, "Dr. Harrold showed me how the top speed is self-limiting because as speed increases the back pressure builds and this tends to increase the load and thus limit speed." That's telling what happened. *Show* it instead, so that the reader can visualize what you saw. Put it this way: "Dr. Harrold walked over and punched a button to start the engine. He opened the throttle and the engine let out a roar. But as speed increased rapidly, he pointed to the back-pressure gauge mounted on a bracket just over the engine. 'Now watch how it rises,' he said. 'As we get to the critical speed, you will see that ... etc." Many of the amateurishly written articles we get are essentially exposition. Avoid this approach. Pack your article with lively quotes, anecdotes, stories, description, narration, reactions.

Popular Science looks for articles which contain three sections: *the lead* (which may involve any of the main types of leads: the narrative lead; the anecdotal lead; the question lead and so on); the establishing section and a *development section.*

They define their second, or establishing section as a section which:
tells clearly and succinctly what the article will be about. It also gives the news peg—why we're bring up this subject now. (A few *Popular Science* articles—principally how-to articles—do not contain news pegs. Most do.) It outlines all territory to be covered, sets boundaries, tells what the article will be about. It prepares the reader to understand the material to follow without having to wonder what point the writer is trying to make. Once the reader has read the establishing section,

nothing in the article will surprise or confuse him. He will never say, "What's the point of all this stuff he's telling me?" or "How does that relate to the subject?" When the reader has read a well-constructed establishing section, the meaning of each subsequent part of the article is clear and he will see the building blocks fall into place one after the other. He understands why they are all there and their interrelationship *as he reads the article.*

The editors also write:

The major reason we have to do heavy rewriting of many articles is that the writer has not analyzed his article and its construction to make sure that the three essential sections are all present.

The last section, or the development section, is defined as:

The third element in a *Popular Science* story—which makes up all the rest after the lead and the establishing section—is the development. This is 90 percent of the article, and it is the part where the writer presents his material, supporting the theme he set forth in the establishing section. This material should be presented in a clearly organized and logical way that will justify the theme stated in the establishing section.

The editors of *Popular Science* also offer their potential contributors a list of guidelines, "Rules, principles, tips." These are not only valid for contributors to *Popular Science,* but also valuable (perhaps invaluable) for all article writers interested in the science fact article:

* Use simple, direct, declarative sentences. Sentences that begin with a dependent clause are not absolutely forbidden, but should be minimized or avoided. The same goes for sentences with complex structure. A good guideline: If a sentence has complex punctuation it is probably too complicated and should be broken up.

* Use anecdotes, narration, quotes, description, first person as much as possible.

* Use exposition as sparingly as you can.

* Show, don't tell. Don't explain to the reader what was going on. Describe it so that he can picture it in his mind. Thus, instead of being vague and theoretical, the subject becomes concrete and far easier for him to grasp and deal with.

* Avoid the use of the first-person plural. While there is nothing technically wrong with such usage, it tends to sound textbookish and patronizing. "Now, students, if we look at the board, we will see that to our left is . . . etc." There's almost always a better way to put it.

Writing the Science Article

* Avoid the use of the word "scientist." Say chemist, physicist, meterologist. Often writers say scientist when they actually mean engineer. There is a difference. Be precise.

* A simple rule on cliches. Don't use them. Ever.

* Do your research. You can't write a *Popular Science* article with information from the library. You've got to be on the scene to get the descriptions, the first-person feel, the good quotes and anecdotes that are so important.

* Once you bring up a certain aspect of a subject, say everything you're going to say about it and drop it. *Do not bring it up again.* This is a cardinal rule of magazine article writing and organization, but one we often see violated. If you find later in a piece that you must bring up a subject a second time, there is something wrong with your original organization. Referring repeatedly to the same point is very confusing to the reader, who is thinking that he has seen this before, but now isn't sure. Was it some slightly different point you discussed before? To be sure, he has to go back and read it again. We have seen the same subject brought up in three or four different places in a single piece. This means that the writer simply has not given enough thought to the organization to put this piece of information in its proper niche.

* Prepare the reader for everything you're going to say so that he understands every statement *when you make it*. We often see pieces in which a writer will do an acceptable lead and establishing section. It tells, for example, that there is an important new engine that uses a new method of carburetion to get both better fuel mileage and lower emissions. Then he will launch into a series of quotes from engineers commenting on certain aspects of its operation that have not yet been introduced. Following these comes the explanation of the principle in question. To understand this, the reader has to hold in his mind the quotes until he is given the explanation that makes them understandable. Obviously, the elements should be in reverse order; the explanation should be given first, then the quotes. Now the reader has the background and the quotes make sense. This is an extremely common error.

* Use a tape recorder. Some writers don't. They should. Transcribing hours of tape into a usable form is a terrible job, but it's worth it. There is no other way you can get the colorful quotes or have as good a grasp of the details of the subject. When I am early in the research process and don't understand as much as I will about the subject when I'm through, I often

THE HARDEST PARTS

fail to understand the significance of something an interview subject says. If I were taking notes, I wouldn't make a note of it at all. Later, when I understand more, I see why an element that seemed unimportant at first is actually critical. And a tape recorder is absolutely essential for getting the really good quotes. The ones you reconstruct from scanty notes are never as fresh and interesting as the original.

* Anecdotes should give enough detail to convince the reader that the story is real, not made up. Take this example:

"A man towing a trailer behind his car pulled off the turnpike and stopped in front of a restaurant one hot day last summer. When he came back out, his car wouldn't start. A mechanic who examined it found that the engine had become so hot that the oil had solidified in the pan and the engine had seized.

"This problem, while fairly rare, is getting more common. And it's one of the reasons that the oil companies have launched into the development of new high-temperature-resistant oil . . . etc."

Somehow, this just doesn't carry the sound of conviction. It sounds made up. Try this instead:

"One sizzling day last summer, Harry Milliam pulled his '72 Buick Wildcat with a trailer hooked on behind into the truck stop on Interstate 20 just easy of Big Spring, Texas. After a quick lunch, he crawled behind the wheel and tried the starter. The engine wouldn't turn over.

"A mechanic on duty made the obvious checks and found nothing wrong, then dropped the oil pan. 'Look at this,' he said, as he stuck a screwdriver into the rubbery mass solidified there. The combination of 95° Texas heat and the extra load of the trailer hauling had pushed the engine temperature above the 300° mark and the oil had turned to muck. When the engine stopped, it solidified into something resembling rubber and the engine seized.

"This problem, while fairly rare, is getting more common . . . etc." Don't overdo detail, but give enough to be convincing.

* Don't confuse simplicity with superficiality. Remember that many *Popular Science* readers are technically sophisticated. While each article must be clear and simple enough so that readers who know nothing about a field can understand it, the article must not oversimplify to the point of being misleading. And it must not patronize the reader. It is difficult to write a clear, accurate description of some very complex physical principle or mechanical operation. It takes even more skill to

do it journalistically, using all the devices of description, narration, quotes, and anecdotes. But it can be done. And that's the kind of writing we're looking for.

* Quote the source—not yourself. We often see something like this. "How did you get the idea in the first place?" I asked Smith. He told me that it had come to him when he was trying to see if he could solve a transmission slippage problem in a new kind of gear assembly he was working on.

It should go this way: I asked Smith how he got the idea: "I was having a problem with a transmission back in the summer of 1977," he said. "It was slipping . . . etc."

* Never say "those of you." Say "you." You are only talking to one reader—the one reading your piece at any time. Address your remarks to him alone.

* If you need more direction—
  If the story line isn't clear enough—
  If the story you proposed and we accepted turns out not to be the real story at all once you get on the scene—
Call and talk it over with us before proceeding. We're always glad to discuss these things on the phone. Stories do change. Things we understood to be true often turn out not to be. New developments often change a story line drastically. Call and talk it over if this happens to you.

* Send out checking copies. Some writers feel that letting a source see a copy of an article before publication is somehow demeaning. We don't think so. No matter how careful you are, small mistakes or misleading ideas can creep in. Having an authority (or several authorities) check the manuscript can catch them before they're committed to type. Make it clear to your source that you are submitting the copy only to find factual error, not for routine editing, changing active to passive verbs, and so on. You may have a fight from time to time with a source who doesn't like what you have to say and will make a fuss to try to have it changed. In the long run, you'll catch enough errors to make this occasional inconvenience worth it.

Suggested reading:

Ward, Ritchie, "How to Write the Science Story." *Writer's Digest,* Feb., 1982.

Chapter Eighteen

Feature Techniques for Television and Radio Reporters

by Gale Wiley

Two distinct trends in journalism make this chapter possible. As more and more magazines and newspapers ask reporters to write simpler, tighter features—"Write for the eye and ear," say editors—more and more radio and television stations are asking *their* writers to produce more "print type" features with added depth and detail. The result is magazine features with more graphics and pictures than ever before. Some magazines have even turned their articles into extended captions. Meanwhile, radio and television stations are pushing for longer, more detailed features written in "magazine format."

Both media, it seems to me, want what the other appears to lack. Electronic media, in its rush for "meaningful journalism," wants the "depth" of print; and print, in its rush to capture readers lost to the tube, wants the "immediacy" of electronics.

The danger of these trends, of course, is that features in both media will become so bastardized that neither will retain its best qualities. Print features *allow* for detail and subtle relationships. Print features require an active participation—and imagination—from the reader. The reader has to spend this imagination to earn the copy's message. Yet the end product, if the copy is well written, is a strong, clear communication between reader and text. Take away description and detail and complexities and you have thrown away the print feature's strongest suit. In broadcast features, however, the viewer/listener plays a more passive role. It is ambience and a sense of NOW that make the broadcast feature successful. Overwrite or provide too much detail or description and you lose the best quality of the broadcast feature.

Gale Wiley worked as a foreign correspondent in West Germany for 11 years and wrote for United Press International, Mutual Radio, National Public Radio and Cox Newspapers, among others. He now teaches at the University of Texas at Austin where he occasionally free-lances for local television stations and produces video productions for corporations.

The trick in writing or broadcast media is understanding the limitations and strengths of each media and working within those boundaries. A free-lance article writer considering a radio feature should listen to radio features and study their form. A newspaper reporter being lured to work for a local television station should look long at the constraints of TV news (its length and reliance on pictures) before he or she takes the job.

And yet, having said all this, print and broadcast features do have much in common. That's why this chapter on broadcast features is tucked at the end of a book on print features. The process of generating ideas, doing research, conducting interviews, writing leads, organizing the copy is basically the same for broadcast and print feature writers. The key to understanding feature writing for radio and television is understanding that print and electronic journalism do have a lot in common, yet success in both requires a clear understanding of their differences.

Broadcast Feature Defined

Print journalist William Ruehlmann writes that a feature "is a hunk of overhead humanity that may or may not have the news value of the large events . . . on the front page." The feature, says Ruehlmann, attempts "to engage or amuse" and at its best even "inform." Feature writers use the techniques of fiction and rely less on formula writing than hard-news writers. Good feature writing, says Ruehlmann, "attempts to provide a moving picture in prose of something real."

In their book "Writing and Reporting Broadcast News," E. Joseph Broussard and Jack F. Holgate say much the same: features "are people stories . . . designed to stir emotions, to stimulate, to divert, to inform, and to entertain." Features on radio and television, write Broussard and Holgate, should be creative and without formula. They should "make the commonplace attractive . . . provide a new perspective to the ordinary, and . . . bring the unusual to the attention of . . . (the) audience."

Nearly all print and broadcast experts agree, too, that features can be classified into basic types. Most typical is the *news feature,* built on a "news peg." The news feature takes a longer look at a headline item. It examines a personality behind a lead story. It provides detail, the "why" of an event. Other features—*profiles*—focus on people: famous or infamous, local or distant, brilliant or inane. Features examine *places,* too: carnivals and churches, classrooms and canneries. Features zero in on *unusual jobs, bizarre events, seasonal changes, future problems,* and much, much more. All features should feature; they spotlight and entertain. And always with personality and flair. They bring the event closer to the audience.

Features are not documentaries. Features are usually part of a longer program while documentaries stand alone. Features are generally shorter

THE HARDEST PARTS

and lighter than documentaries with less research and a freer structure. Investigative pieces are not features, either. Generally, the investigative broadcast story is just another name for a documentary.

While the distinctions between these broadcast forms are not always crystal clear, techniques for creating them are the same. Generating the idea, searching for clips and books and interview subjects, conducting the interviews, and finding a lead and structure for the piece are routine steps for any feature—print or broadcast. But the broadcast writer has several additional problems that do not face the print writer.

Key Differences

• *Actualities.* At the same time the broadcast reporter/writer takes notes with an interview subject, he or she must make sure that key quotes get on tape. In the case of television that means in-focus, well-lighted visuals with clear sound of important passages. In radio than means tape devoid of disrupting background noise, a voice "on mike." These interviews on tape are what broadcasters call "actualities," "sound bites," "taking heads," and "cuts." These are equivalents to the quotations that appear in the print article.

• *Writing.* "Words written for television are meant to be heard by the ear, not seen by the eye," writes Andy Rooney in his best-selling book *A Few Minutes With Andy Rooney.* "At best it (television writing) comes out as a compromise between written and spoken English. To be spoken aloud, the sentences have to be shorter and the writing simpler. If it is concentrated and there are ideas in the writing, it has to be slowed down because all of us talk faster than we listen . . . ."

Generally, journalism professors like to point out that a typical daily paper may contain 100,000 words or more of copy while the average half hour TV newscast contains only some 4,000 words. And yet both have the same newsday to report. But that's only half the story.

Pictures contain vast amounts of information, too, huge blocks of images which taken together with sound produce a synergistic effect *and* much more information than 4,000 words. An angry voice, a shaking fist and a raised eyebrow obviously have more impact when we *see and hear* them than when we *read* them.

The trick in television writing is thinking visually, realizing that visual information has a logic and impact, that words take second place to pictures. Writing in the present tense, allowing for a certan amount of redundancy, cutting out too many details are other rules.

The broadcast feature writer must use actualities carefully. Narration should serve as a bridge between actualities. It should set themes, lead the audience and give a feeling of organization and shape.

• *Technology.* Broadcast writers must understand the technology of broadcasting—not the complex circuitry but the mechanics of editing audio and videotape, the mechanics of producing a radio and television show, the theory of mixing and dubbing. They must understand how to operate a camera and tape recorder.

They must know the limitations of equipment, too, how it works under what conditions. They must understand what happens step-by-step with a piece of freshly recorded videotape. They must know what to do when the camera or tape recorder suddenly breaks down.

In short, the images must be in focus and the sound must be audible and crisp. Otherwise, the broadcast journalist has no feature.

• *Editing.* The print feature writer checks her notes and finds a quotation. But it's too long. She simply lops out a few words without distorting the meaning, and she taps out the quote. Easy.

But the broadcast writer doesn't have this luxury. With videotape an editor cannot easily lop away "ah's" and "oh's" and awkward phrasing. Otherwise the image results in something called a "jump cut," the speaker sounding okay but the picture jumping across the edit. An editor can insert something called a "cutaway" (a shot of the reporter asking the question or a shot of the reporter and newsmaker together to fill the space left by the edit), but there are limits to how many cutaways an editor can do.

Audio tape for radio features is generally easier to edit, thus allowing an editor to make most everyone speak efficiently, without pause or hesitation. Even verbal ticks like "you know" can be eliminated. Chunks of tape from different points in an interview can be assembled to focus on specific themes.

But ethically there are problems with broadcast editing. In television there is always the possibility that an unethical producer inserts a different question to an answer. In radio, two pieces of distant tape can be used together to create an impression that does not necessarily reflect a subject's meaning. On the other hand, good editing can focus on compress reality, helping to communicate complicated ideas efficiently.

• *Time.* Finally, there is the constraint of deadline pressure coupled with the fact that one's feature has been given only two minutes air time. Print features generally allow for more writing time, but broadcast features are generally done under the gun. Great bites of actualities and detail end up unused. Images are tightened to mere seconds on the screen. What had been a string of details now becomes a fleeting image.

• *Translation.* Broadcast pieces do not necessarily make great print features and vice versa. They usually lose something in the translation from media to media, but every day at radio and television stations across the country reporters find newspaper stories that yield feature ideas. Sometimes the feature is faithful to the article, but most of the time the broadcast feature becomes something quite different, another story

THE HARDEST PARTS

altogether.

Susan Stamberg of National Public Radio's "All Things Considered" writes that "converting radio into print has its limitations. You lose the laughs . . . the silences . . . the music of voices . . . the music of bands, kazoos, synthesizers. By definition, the purest radio pieces don't translate into type."

But many do.

A useful exercise for the writer interested in broadcast features is translating print features to broadcast features. A good way to start such an exercise is an examination of the two chapters on leads (Chapters Eight and Nine) in this book. With an ounce of imaginaton, a writer needs to think of substituting visuals and sounds for what's happening on the printed page.

For example, a descriptive lead instantly translates to videotape. The narrator is off-camera. Descriptive sentences now become pictures. The narrator merely bridges and explains the movement of the pictures, sometimes adding redundancy by putting into words what is on the screen, sometimes explaining the significance of the images. For radio the descriptive sentences which lend themselves to sound *become* sounds.

An anecdotal lead in print becomes a short story, a kind of tiny documentary either staged or reenacted or recorded as it happened. The British Broadcasting System uses this technique on both television and radio to add life to feature stories. A typical BBC beginning for a feature piece on radio might be, "On May 25, 1902, Sir Henry Smith saw a tiny creature working his way across one of his dahlias . . ." And then suddenly, we hear Sir Henry's voice: "I say, what is this?" And so on, the narrator providing bridges for the dialogue.

After practicing translating several print leads into radio and television, then try your hand at an entire feature.

TELEVISION FEATURE

Let's see how one broadcast journalist might handle Tom Fensch's print feature of the Niagara Falls hero (Chapter Two).

Getting story ideas is much the same for print and broadcast reporters. A news editor at a local television station might hand over the same clip Fensch saw about the Hill family to a TV reporter. The young reporter says "OK, how much time?" The editor tells her, "Keep it under a minute fifteen. If it's good, we'll use it as the kicker on the evening show."

Two key differences emerge here. The TV reporter must usually do the story the same day it's assigned. If she's lucky, she will get two or three days. She also must keep the story extremely short. She must cover in one minute, fifteen seconds what the newspaper did in 10 column inches and

Fensch did in some 3,000 words.

The reporter reads the copy. As she does this, she notes possibilities for visuals. She knows that the station has file tape of dramatic rescues made over the last few years, and fatalities. She doesn't know if the station has any footage of the dramatic rescue attempts made by Hill or any of his family.

Her big problem is getting an interview—on tape. She must call the subject immediately and set an interview. She has to arrange for a camera. She also must check for any other information about rescues, stunts, and deaths at Niagara Falls.

She has an hour or so before the interview with Wes Hill, and she decides to spend it at the local library. There she collects the facts, interesting anecdotes, and background.

She knows there is an old film footage of the Falls available at the local historic society. She knows, too, that she can show footage for a dramatic opening—if she can get the film, transfer it to videotape, and have it edited. She tells her editor of her plans. He puts a staffer to work on it.

On the way to Wes Hill's home, the reporter thinks about the possibilities of the story. She imagines an opening with a series of people trying to go over the falls in barrels—old footage of people nearly drowning, bodies floating in the water... a dramatic opening. Cut to Wes Hill along the river, perhaps with a rope, simulating a rescue attempt? Perhaps still photos of Wes and his family together, the camera zooming in on Wes as the only Hill left to do the work of a rescuer?

The reporter casts narration out in her mind . . . "HUNDREDS OF PEOPLE HAVE RISKED THEIR LIVES AT NIAGARA FALLS . . . HUNDREDS MORE HAVE FALLEN VICTIM TO THE FALLS . . . DROWNING, LOSING THEIR BOATS TO THE TUG OF THE STREAM . . . BUT ONE FAMILY, THE HILL FAMILY, IS RESPONSIBLE FOR SAVING MORE THAN 500 LIVES AT THE FALLS . . . ALL OF THE HILLS ARE GONE EXCEPT WES . . . . (tight shot on each family member) . . . WHO IS STILL AT WORK RESCUING PEOPLE, ANIMALS AND EVEN RAFTS . . . " "CUT TO HILL ALONG THE RIVER TALKING ABOUT HIS RESCUE ATTEMPTS . . . "

Our reporter meets Hill. She chats with him amiably as the cameraman sets lights and camera. She notes questions that will bring out solid quotes. Why do you rescue people? How many people have you saved? (The answer to this question will probably be told by the reporter rather than let Hill tell it.) Tell me about the history of your family again, about each generation of Hill and his rescue attempts.

As the clock ticks away our reporter knows she can not cover the story in great detail. She can not possibly tell the whole story, but she knows that

THE HARDEST PARTS

the file footage will help her out. After her interview she calls her station and asks for two more days on this one. She feels she can do more with the feature, make it an even better story. Her editor says, OK, two days max.

She asks Hill to go to the river. She wants footage of him with the Falls in the background, working with his sons practicing a rescue. She wants to get footage of old clippings too. She asks Hill for any old newspapers or magazine clippings about his adventures. He produces an album. She brings the album along and copies it at a copy shop. As she works, she keeps the story in her mind. The story replays in her mind's eye, over and over. She must get the shots she needs.

She imagines Wes Hill walking along the river, near the falls. She has the interview with him and she plans to use the audio "over" with shots of him ambling along the river. The effect will be more compression of information. Action and actuality.

Finally, our reporter says she has gathered enough videotape. Back at the studio she reviews a log she has made of all the shots, their lengths, type of shots (close-up, medium close up. establishment shot, etc.) and a short description of each one. This saves her time writing the story. She learns that old file footage from the late 20s and 30s is available. That has been videotaped, too.

This is how she might handle the story, the video description on the left with times shown and the audio on the right column. She decides to record the audio in the studio and then have one of the videotape editors insert the visual material to fit the audio.

VIDEO	AUDIO
VTR—	(Nat. Sound Under: Falls)
Niagara Falls, ext. Black-and-white film from 20s and 30s Series of people shooting Falls Rescuers pulling victim from water	*Reporter:* No one knows exactly how many have shot Niagara Falls in a barrel, but hundreds of people have risked their lives here . . . . and hundreds more have died here, too. In barrels and boats they have risked their lives . . . .
CU Portrait Hill Family	And for more than half a century a family named Hill has either been challenging the Niagara or fighting it trying to save victims of the river.
Ext. CU "Red" Hill Mix with old film	First there was "Red" Hill who shot the lower rapids in a barrel three times over three decades.

Ext. CU "Red" Junior Mix with old film	He saved 28 people and found 177 bodies in the river's waters . . . Then there was "Red" Junior who died trying to shoot the Falls in a contraption called THE THING . . .
Ext. CU Major Hill File film	And "Red" Hill's second son, Major, who shot the lower rapids four times . . .
Ext. Along Niagara MCU Wes Hill	And of a father and four sons, Wes Hill is the only one left . . . .
Hill throwing weighted rope into Niagara River	*Wes Hill* (voice over): When Dad died of a heart attack in 1942, he had taken out 144 bodies. I have helped on almost three hundred myself and my brothers helped, when they were alive. So it's a bit above five hundred now . . .

And so on for the rest of the feature.

RADIO FEATURE

If our reporter had been working for National Public Radio, he might have run across the same newspaper clipping about Wes Hill, but might not have considered old movie footage as a research source. Instead, he would be more interested in interview material gathered into his tape recorder, interviews with local citizens who know the Hill family, interviews with the Hills (Wes and family), the sound of the Falls, sounds of Hill walking along the river, the sound of a dog barking mixed with the river sounds, old radio tape (if any of the local stations have it), and of course a long interview with Wes himself.

This might be one way to do a Wes Hill feature for radio:

(NIAGARA FALLS. FADE AND HOLD UNDER)
WES HILL: I took a few minutes to look for the light and dark places so I could tell where the shallows were. Then I waded into the river . . .
(FALLS, WADING AND DOG BARKING FAINTLY. MIXED AND UNDER)
WES HILL: The rope was weighted at one end. So I'd throw it a bit upstream, pull myself out a ways with it, pull the rope in and throw it again . . .

THE HARDEST PARTS

(BARKING DOG FADE UP AGAINST FALLS AND WADING SOUNDS)
WES HILL: Finally, I worked my way out step-by-step until I reached the dog... he was just full of joy. He kissed and licked my face all the way back.
(FADE UNDER AND OUT)
ANNOUNCER: For Wesley Hill, rescuing a collie dog stranded above Niagara Falls is all in a day's work. After all, his father and grandfather and three brothers spent their lives challenging and fighting the river and its falls... saving hundreds of lives... plucking some 500 bodies from the river, usually at the base of the Falls... and occasionally shooting the falls in a barrel...
OLD RADIO TAPE:
    We're standing at the observation deck here above the Falls and we can see "Red" Hill in his specially-built barrel which he will use to shoot the Falls, falling 327 feet to the rocks below...

    Obviously, a feature writer for radio must make each segment of tape count, recreating the feel of the Falls and at the same time giving hard facts. The piece should include statistics—but not too many. It should show that Wes Hill's family is continuing the tradition of playing sentinel to Niagara Falls as well. Much of the historical material evident in Fensch's piece would be cut from the radio feature. It can not provide as much anecdotal material either. There simply isn't enough time. But if well handled, this radio feature can have as much impact as Tom Fensch's print feature.

Bibliography

Applebaum, Judith and Evans, Nancy. *How to Get Happily Published.* New York: Harper & Row, 1978.

Armour, Richard. "Good References for Writers." *The Writer,* March, 1980.

Baker, Bob. "How to Put Perspective in Your Nonfiction." *Writer's Digest,* Dec., 1981.

_____. "How to Turn Rejects Into Sales." *The Writer,* Feb., 1979.

_____. "Writing Salable Nonfiction." *The Writer,* May, 1972.

Balkin, Richard. *A Writer's Guide to Book Publishing.* New York: Hawthorn Books, 1977.

Behrens, John C. *The Magazine Writer's Workbook.* Columbus, Ohio: Grid, Inc., 1972.

Beinswinger, George L. "The Electronic Freelancer." *Writer's Digest,* April, 1981.

Bernstein, Paul. "Take Care of Your Tape Recorder and It Will Take Care of You." *Writer's Digest,* May, 1979.

Berger, Paul. "A Writer's Guide to Tiny Tape Recorders." *Writer's Digest,* May, 1979.

Brady, John. *The Craft of Interviewing.* Cincinnati: Writer's Digest Books, 1979.

Burroughs, William E. *On Reporting the News.* New York: New York University Press, 1977.

"Computer Checklist." *Writer's Digest,* April, 1981.

Caruana, Claudia M. "A Basic Reference Bookshelf for Writers.' *Writer's Digest,* Oct., 1981.

Casewit, Curtis. *Freelance Writing: Advice from the Pros.* New York: Collier Books (Div. of Macmillan), 1974.

Cassill, Kay. *The Complete Handbook for Freelance Writers.* Cincinnati: Writer's Digest Books, 1981.

Cleaver, Diane. "All About Agents." *Writer's Digest,* June, 1980.

Courter, Gay. "Word Machines for Word People." *Publisher's Weekly,* Feb. 13, 1981.

Curtis, Richard. *How To Be Your Own Literary Agent.* Boston: Houghton Mifflin Co., 1983.

Daigh, Ralph. *Maybe You Should Write a Book.* Englewood Cliffs, N.J.: Prentice-Hall, 1977.

Deken, Joseph. *The Electronic Cottage.* New York: William Morrow, 1981.

Dickson, Frank A. *1001 Article Ideas.* Cincinnati: Writer's Digest Books, 1979.

_____. *Writer's Digest Handbook of Article Writing.* New York: Holt, Rinehart & Winston, 1968.
Duncan, Lois. "How to Write Your Way Through College." *The Writer,* Feb., 1976.
Edel, Leon. *Literary Biography.* Bloomington: The University of Indiana Press, rev. ed., 1973.
Elliott, Osborn. *The World of Oz.* New York: The Viking Press, 1980.
Evans, Glen, ed., *The Complete Guide to Writing Nonfiction.* Cincinnati, O., Writer's Digest Books, 1984.
Everett, Betty Steele. "Article Ideas Unlimited." *The Writer,* March, 1980.
Fallows, James. "Living with a Computer." *The Atlantic Monthly,* July, 1982.
Fensch, Thomas. *Steinbeck and Covici: The Story of a Friendship.* Middlebury, Vt.: Paul S. Eriksson, Inc., 1979.
_____. "Tapping the University Community Market." *Writer's Digest,* March, 1969.
_____. "Turning Articles Into Books." *Writer's Digest,* Dec., 1969.
Fisher, Jonathan. "Writing Article Queries That Sell." *The Writer,* June, 1971.
Fontaine, Andre. *The Art of Writing Nonfiction.* New York: Thomas Crowell, 1974.
Gehman, Richard. *How to Write and Sell Magazine Articles.* New York: Harper & Bro., 1959.
Gill, Betsy. *Magazine Article Writing: Substance and Style.* New York: Holt, Rinehart & Winston, 1980.
Gunther, Max. "Article Research by Mail." *The Writer,* Aug., 1979.
_____. "Interviewing for Nonfiction Writing." *The Writer,* May, 1973.
_____. "Using Quotes in Nonfiction Writing." *The Writer,* Sept. 1978.
_____. "When You Need a Nonfiction Idea." *The Writer,* Jan., 1976.
_____. "Writing the Query Letter." *The Writer,* Sept., 1972.
Hallstead, William F. "How to Write a Query Letter." *The Writer,* Aug., 1976.
Hartley, William B. "Building the Magazine Article." *The Writer,* Sept., 1981.
Henry, Omer. "Nonfiction Salesmanship." *The Writer,* Dec., 1978.
Hensley, Dennis E. "Getting Impossible-to-Get Interviews." *The Writer,* June, 1980.
Holden, Larry. "The Three R's for Revitalizing Article Sales." *Writer's Digest,* Jan., 1980.

Holmes, Marjarie. *Writing the Creative Article.* Boston: The Writer, Inc., 1973.

Horowitz, Lois. "The Writer's Guide to Periodical Literature." *Writer's Digest,* Oct., 1981.

Jacobs, Hayes B. *A Complete Guide to Writing and Selling Non-fiction.* Cincinnati: Writer's Digest Books, 1967.

Jacobson, Emilie. "The Literary Agent and the Freelance Writer." *The Writer,* July, 1972.

Johnson, Tom. "Four for the Future." *Writer's Digest,* April, 1981.

Kelley, Jerome E. *Magazine Writing Today.* Cincinnati: Writer's Digest Books, 1978.

Lampe, David. "Unloved and Unloving, the Armadillo Blunders On." *National Wildlife,* Feb.-March, 1977.

Literary Market Place. New York: R. R. Bowker, Inc. (Various editions; annual directory.)

MacCampbell, Donald. *The Writing Business.* New York: Crown Publishers, 1978.

Mayer, Suzanne. "Diary of a First Article." *The Writer,* Aug., 1972.

Metzler, Ken. *Creative Interviewing.* Englewood Cliffs, N.J.: Prentice-Hall, Inc., 1977.

Miller, Bobby Ray, ed. *United Press International Stylebook.* New York: United Press International, 1977.

Miles, William E. "Article Outlines Bring Sales." *The Writer,* Feb., 1982.

Miller, Casey and Swift, Kate. *The Handbook of Nonsexist Writing for Writers, Editors and Speakers.* New York: Lippincott & Crowell, 1980.

Mogel, Leonard. *The Magazine: Everything You Need to Know to Make It in the Magazine Business.* Englewood Cliffs, N.J.: Prentice-Hall, 1979.

Morris, Terry, Farb, Peter and Weisinger, Mort. *Prose by Professionals.* Garden City: Doubleday, 1961.

Mueller, William Behr. "How to Pre-Sell an Editor." *The Writer,* Aug., 1978.

Nelson, Roy Paul. *Articles and Features.* Boston: Houghton Mifflin, Inc., 1978.

Newcomb, Duane. *A Complete Guide to Marketing Magazine Articles.* Cincinnati: Writer's Digest Books, 1975.

Newman, Edwin. *A Civil Tongue.* Indianapolis: Bobbs-Merrill, 1976.

_____. *Strictly Speaking: Will America Be the Death of English?* Indianapolis: Bobbs-Merrill, 1974.

Olds, Sally Wendkos. "Write a Query—Get an Assignment." *The Writer,* Aug., 1977.

Olfson, Lewy. "Building Yourself an Idea Factory." *The Writer*, April, 1979.

Pachter, Marc, ed. *Telling Lives: The Biographer's Art*. Washington, D.C.: New Republic Books, 1979.

Patterson, Helen M. *Writing and Selling Feature Articles*. Englewood Cliffs, N.J.: Prentice-Hall, Inc., 3rd rev. ed. 1956.

Perlmutter, Jerome H. *A Practical Guide to Effective Writing*. New York: Delta Books, 1965.

Perry, Robin. "A Writer's Guide to Word Processors." *Writer's Digest*, April, 1981.

Pesta, Ben. "Writing the Query Letter." *The Writer*, July, 1975.

Peterson, Theodore. *Magazines in the Twentieth Century*. Urbana, Ill.: The University of Illinois Press, 1964.

Polking, Kirk, Chimsky, Jean and Adkins, Rose. *The Beginning Writer's Answer Book*. Cincinnati: Writer's Digest Books, 2nd rev. ed., 1978.

Poynter, Margaret. "How an Article Idea Grows." *The Writer*, Oct., 1978.

Provost, Gary. "Writing and Selling the Personality Profile." *Writer's Digest*, Nov., 1981.

Reddick, DeWitt. *Modern Feature Writing*. New York: Harper & Bro., 1949.

Rivers, William L. *Finding Facts: Interviewing, Observing, Using Reference Sources*. Englewood Cliffs, N.J.: Prentice-Hall, 1975.

_____. *Writing: Craft and Art*. Englewood Cliffs, N.J.: Prentice-Hall, 1975.

Rivers, William L. and Smolkin, Shelly. *FreeLancer and Staff Writer: Newspaper Features and Magazine Articles*. Belmont, Calif.: Wadsworth Publishing Co., 3rd ed. 1981.

Reynolds, Paul R. *The Middle Man*. New York: William Morrow, 1972.

Ruehlmann, William. *Stalking the Feature Story*. Cincinnati: Writer's Digest Books, 1978.

Secrest, Meryl. "The Story of a Life." *The Writer*, June, 1981.

"Should You Really Have an Agent?" *The Writer*, July, 1971.

Smith, Kay. "From Amateur to Pro in the Article Market." *The Writer*, April, 1970.

Sokolov, Raymond. *Wayward Reporter: The Life of A.J. Liebling*. New York: Harper & Row, 1980.

Spikol, Art. *Magazine Writing: The Inside Angle*. Cincinnati: Writer's Digest Books, 1979.

_____. "Nonfiction: Getting Booked." *Writer's Digest*, May, 1979.

_____. "Nonfiction: Postal Mortem." *Writer's Digest*, Nov., 1979.

Strunk, William and White, E.B. *Elements of Style.* New York: Macmillan, 3rd ed., 1979.
Swanson, Marshall. "Covering the Campus." *Writer's Digest,* May, 1979.
Taft, William H. *American Magazines for the 1980s.* New York: Hastings House, 1982.
"The *Writer's Digest* Top 100 Markets." *Writer's Digest,* Jan., 1982.
Vandervoort, Paul II. "How to Get an Article Idea." *The Writer,* May, 1976.
Ward, Ritchie. "How to Write the Science Story." *Writer's Digest,* Feb., 1978.
Webb, Eugene and Solancik, Jerry R. "The Interview or the Only Wheel in Town." *Journalism Monographs,* No. 2, Nov., 1966.
Weisinger, Mort. "Titles That Talk." *The Writer,* Aug., 1975.
Williams, W.P. and Van Zandt, Joseph H. *How to Write Magazine Articles That Sell.* Chicago: Contemporary Books, 1979.
Wolseley, Roland E. *The Changing Magazine: Trends in Readership and Management.* New York: Hastings House, 1973.
_____. *Understanding Magazines.* Ames, Iowa: Iowa State University Press, 2nd ed., 1969.
Writer's Markets. Cincinnati: Writer's Digest Books. (Various editions, annual directory.)
Zinsser, William. *On Writing Well.* New York: Harper & Row, 1980.

Glossary

Angle: The point-of-view focus or emphasis in an article.

Annual: Yearly special or extra issue devoted to seasonal subject, such as a Christmas annual (issue).

Art: Illustrations, drawings diagram or other non-print material which accompanies an article; common name for all non-textual material.

Assignment: Any specific task given to an individual; i.e., a commissioned article assignment to a free-lancer by a magazine.

Author's Alternations (AA's): Changes or corrections made by the writer in textual material (usually in galley proof form) before the material is printed.

Back issue: Any issue of a magazine or newspaper printed prior to the current-date (news-stand) issue.

Back-of-the-Book: Secondary articles, columns and other material literally or figuratively printed behind the primary articles.

Back shop: Composing room area of newspaper.

Bingo card: Postage-paid insert in a magazine which readers can complete and return to begin a magazine subscription. So called because they are often the size of bingo playing cards.

Bleed: To run an illustration past the margins to the edges of a page.

Blue-pencil: Slang for editing corrections. So-named because blue pencil or ink can't be photographed by photo-offset cameras.

Blurb: Short description of an article or subject.

Body (of the article): The core of an article; i.e., material following the lead segment.

Book: Industry slang for *magazine*. So-named—perhaps—because some monthly dummies are the sizes of books.

By-line: A line of type published before or after an article identifying the author.

Camera Ready: Material which has been corrected and is ready to be photographed for photo-offset printing.

Caption: Material which explains the contents of a photograph or illustration. Sometimes called *art lines* or *cut lines*.

Center Spread: The two facing pages at the exact center of a magazine, i.e., center.

Circulation: The number of copies of a magazine or newspaper printed, distributed or sold during a specific period.

Clean copy: Pristine text, unmarred by many editing symbols. Opposite of *dirty copy*.

Close (Closing date): The deadline for all material for a newspaper or magazine to be on the press.

Cold type: Material prepared for printing without hot metal; i.e., Linotype machines.
Commission: Same as *to assign an article.*
Contents Page: Page usually near the front of a magazine which lists the contents of the issue.
Copy: All written material in manuscript form which will eventually be considered for publication.
Copyeditor: Person who reads, and corrects all copy prior to publication.
Copyright: The legal ownership of a manuscript.
Cover: The outside front page, inside front page, inside rear page and outside rear page of a magazine: *to cover,* to gather all the facts necessary for an article.
Crop: To mark un-wanted sections of a photograph or illustration.
Cut (noun): A metal engraving of an illustration; *to cut* (verb): to edit material.
Cutlines: Same as *caption* or *art lines.*
Dateline: Line on an article giving the location and date the article originated; i.e., Washington, Feb. 23 . . .
Dead: Material that has been *killed;* i.e., material which will not be printed.
Deadline: Time when all material to be published must be written, copyedited and ready for the press.
Department: Specific section of a magazine, involving special features or area of interest.
Dirty copy: Material which has been heavily copy-edited such that it is illegible; opposite of *clean copy.*
Double-spread: Two facing pages treated as one unit.
Dummy: Planning or proof pages for an issue which has not yet been printed; a checking copy to make sure changes and corrections have been made to a particular issue.
Edition: Same as *issue.*
Editor: Person who reads, changes or verifies all material and makes it ready for publication, in a newspaper or magazine.
Editorial Content: All non-advertising material in a newspaper or magazine; the literary contents of a publication.
Editorialize: To express a position or opinion on behalf of the publication, as in an editorial or a publisher's or editor's column.
Editor's Note: Material which helps explain an article or author or position which a publication has taken on an issue.
Engraving: Same as *cut.*
Feature (noun): A human-interest article; *to feature* (verb), to emphasize or give permanence to.
Filler: Incidental (usually short) material which is used to complete columns or pages.

THE HARDEST PARTS

Flag: The name of a newspaper or magazine recognizable not only by name, but also by design; i.e., the Gothic flag of *The New York Times.*
Format: The size, design and appearance of a magazine.
Four-color: Pages which are printed in the colors of red-yellow, blue and black inks.
Free Lance: Person who contributes articles, photographs or any other material without the security of a staff salary.
Front-of-the-book: Articles of primary importance literally or figuratively printed at the front of the magazine.
Galley proof: Vertical column of material typeset for checking purposes.
Gatefold: A page in a magazine which is larger than the normal page and which must be folded to fit inside the magazine; i.e., the *Playboy* Playmate-of-the-Month pages.
General magazine: Any magazine edited and published for a wide reading audience, all ages, interests, religions, etc. *Life* and *The Saturday Evening Post* are examples. Opposite of special-interest magazine.
Ghost Writer: Person who writes material which will eventually be published under the name of another person.
Graf (or *Graph*): Short for *Paragraph.*
Gutter: The inside margins of pages.
Handout: Publicity release.
Head: Headline.
Horizontal magazine: Same as *general magazine.*
Hot type: Material prepared with hot metal; i.e., Linotype machines. Opposite of *cold type* or photo-offset composition.
House ad: Advertisement which promotes the same newspaper or magazine which published it.
House organ: Publication issued by a commercial firm to promote interest in the firm by employees, stockholders or the public.
HTK: Head to come; headline not yet ready.
Human interest: Feature article with emotional appeal to the reader; different than straight news which is presumably tone-less in content.
Insert: Material which has to be added to the inside of a previously-completed article, or specially prepared advertising supplement to a newspaper or magazine.
Inventory: Material on hand in a magazine or newspaper office which may be used at any time.
Issue: Same as *edition.*
Italic: Script type which slants to the right, like handwriting. Italic type is often used to emphasize or highlight material.
Jump: To continue a story from one page to another or from one section to another.

Jump Head: Headline over the second or continued part of a story.

Keep Standing: Material that is held in a newspaper or magazine's inventory, opposite of *kill.*

Kill: To delete material set for publication.

Kill fee (Kill rate): Payment made to a writer after an article is assigned, completed, then killed by a magazine. The kill rate or kill fee is usually a percentage of the fee paid for a published article. The writer usually retains legal rights to material killed by a publication.

Layout: The design of a page including textual material, or art which will later be published.

Lead: Beginning segment of an article.

Libel: A defamatory statement or representation published without just cause, expressed in print or by pictures, that exposes another to public hatred, contempt or ridicule.

Linotype: Trade name for a key-board operated typesetting machine, which produces a line of type in the form of a metal slug.

Little magazine: Small circulation magazines, often less than 8½" x 11", which contain poetry, fiction or avant garde material. Because of lack of advertising or subscription-base, little magazines often die quickly. They are the publishing equivalent of the Mayfly.

Localize: To stress the local angle of a story.

Logo: Same as flag or masthead.

Magazine: Regularly issued publication which contain fiction, non-fiction, and art which is aimed at a specific reading public; carries the original definition of powdermagazine; i.e., storehouse.

Makeup: The consistent of a total publication.

Mark up: To edit copy and make corrections on galley proofs.

Market: The audience for a magazine or publication.

Masthead: Material usually printed toward the front of a magazine, which lists title, editors and staff members, address and subscription rates.

More: Used at the bottom of a page, often in parenthesis, to indicate there are additional pages to the article.

Morgue: Newspaper or magazine library or files.

Ms: Manuscript.

Must: Material so marked has a high priority and should be printed.

Nameplate: Same as *flag* or *logo.*

Non-fiction: Material based on facts; not fiction.

Obit: Obituary, biography of recently-deceased person.

Offset: Printing process in which an inked impression is made on a rubber "blanket" and then transferred or "offset" to paper.

OK for press: notation meaning: Can now be printed.

Op-Ed page: The right-hand page opposite or facing the editorial page. Many metropolitan newspapers use the Op-Ed page as a continuation of editorials, essays, letters-to-the-editor and other allied material.

On-sale date: Date on which a particular issue is available for sale throughout the publication's circulation area.

One-shot book: Magazine which has only one planned issue. One-shot books are often published after the death of a President, or the Pope or other famous or notorious people.

There were a variety of One-shot books published after the death of Elvis Presley.

On spec (On speculation): Any material written and submitted for publication without prior financial agreements with a magazine.

Outline: Topic-by-topic skeleton of an article.

Overset: Material which has been set in type but not used by a newspaper or magazine.

Over-the-transom: Unsolicited material which is submitted to a magazine which must be sorted, read, bought or returned. (Some magazines will not read over-the-transom material because of the costs of staff member's time to read and reply to it.) Over-the-transom material becomes part of the magazine's *slush pile.*

Pad: To lengthen with additional material.

Periodical: Publication issued at regular intervals longer than one day; i.e., magazines, not newspapers.

Personality piece: Biography of a person in magazine form.

Pics or *Pix:* Pictures.

Piece: Slang for *article.*

Play up: To emphasize.

Policy: Official viewpoint of a magazine as stated in editorial, columns or other features; i.e., "The Playboy Philosophy," a series in *Playboy* written by publisher Hugh Hefner.

Profile: Personality article.

Promotion: Active campaign to enhance the acceptance and sale of a newspaper or magazine.

Proof: Copy of material used for checking and correcting purposes.

Proofread: To check such material prior to publication.

Pulp: Magazines printed on cheap newspring; often carried the connotation of sensational material.

Put to bed: To put on press; to close an issue.

Query letter: Letter from a freelance writer outlining an article idea and asking for an acceptance from a magazine on the idea.

Quote: Quotation.

Readability: The ease by which a story can be read; visually, pertains to legibility and design of article or layout.

Readership: Surveyed or estimated audience of a magazine; not the same as circulation.

Regional advertisements: Advertisements which appear in issues of a magazine for a particular region.

Rejection slip: Small letter sent to freelancers with articles which a magazine has decided not to buy.

Reprint: Article printed separately and sent to readers or advertisers after the article has first appeared in print. Scholarly magazines often sell reprints to authors for their own distribution. Or: an article which had appeared previously in another publication.

Researcher: Editorial staff member who supplies facts necessary for an article or who verifies facts in an article. Slang term for researcher is *checker,* in news magazines.

Resume: Summary of education, and experience, sent by individual to prospective employers.

Rewrite: To write manuscript again.

Rim: Edge of copy desk, where editors check material.

Rough: Full-sized sketch of layout.

Roundup: Article which is largely summary in nature.

Running head: headline which gives magazine title, date, volume and page, printed at the top of magazine pages.

Running story: Story which is continuing and which may demand follow-up articles on a day-to-day or week-to-week basis.

SASE: Self-addressed stamped envelope. Many magazines require a writer to enclose an SASE to receive an answer to a query. The writer is, in effect, paying for the return postage.

Scoop (noun): Exclusive material;
    (verb): to scoop, to beat the competition.

Seasonal story: An article emphasizing a season, holiday or celebration. Must be prepared well in advance, sometimes as much as a half-year in advance for monthly magazines.

Shelter books: Magazines related to the home.

Sister publications: Magazines which are published by one firm: *Time, Life, Fortune, Money, People,* and *Sports Illustrated* are all sister publications, published by Time, Inc.

Sidebar: A smaller story which accompanies a larger story.

Slant: To emphasize a particular aspect of a story.

Slick: A magazine printed on high-gloss heavy paper. Common industry term for mass circulation consumer magazines.

Slug: Abbreviated headline used to identify each story; in hot metal composition, a line of type.

Slush pile: Unsolicited manuscripts which arrive at magazine editorial offices and which must be sorted, read, accepted or returned.

Solicit: Commission an article, photographs or other material from

THE HARDEST PARTS

contributors.

Special-interest books: Magazines which are edited for a special subsection of the population; those interested in a particular hobby, craft, etc.

Split run: A press run which is stopped to change an advertisement.

Staffer: Magazine staff member, writer, researcher, editor, etc.

Style: A writer's individual expression through the special use of grammar, spelling, punctuation, point of view.

Summary lead: A lead which generally covers most of the "5 W's and the H": who, what, when, where, why and how.

Syndicate: Organization which sells photographs or textual material to a variety of publications. A journalism wholesaler.

Taboo: Words, phrases or subjects which cannot be published for moral or legal reasons.

Take: One page of copy. As more and more publications are written and edited on computers, *take* is likely to fade from writers' vocabularies. Originated (perhaps) in earlier years when a fast-breaking story was *taken* page by page from the writer to the backshop.

Tear sheets: Articles or advertisements torn from a published newspaper or magazine and sent to writers or advertisers to verify that the material (article, ad) was published.

Teaser: Headline or blurb printed on the front cover of a magazine to interest readers in the magazine's content.

Think piece: Interpretative article or essay slanted to make a reader think about the subject. Sometimes condesending term referring to such issues as oil production, taxes, and other hard-to-explain subjects.

Thirty (30): Used on the last page of an article to indicate *the end*.

Tight: Issue which has little room for any additional material.

Title: Same as headline.

TK: Indicates material *to come;* not yet ready.

Typo: Typesetting mistake.

VDT: Video Display Terminal. Typewriter keyboard and television-type screen which allows a writer to compose his story on the keyboard, view it on the screen, edit it and enter it into a computer for storage and retrieval. Electronic storage and publication is said to constitute the third stage of communications, from mechanical to electric to electronic.

Vertical magazine: Same as *special-interest magazine;* not necessarily a magazine which is vertically designed.

White space: Blank spaces on a page, left blank for design purposes.

Work-for-hire: Writing which is assumed by a magazine to be done as staff work. Freelancers who sell material onm a "work-for-hire" basis generally lose all further legal rights to the work.

"XXX": Used in copy to indicate *facts to come* (or needed); "There are XXX automobiles in Russia this year." Newsmagazine usage.

Index

Abex Industries, 11
Acquire: The Magazine of Contemporary Collectibles, 22
Adam, 23
Affair, 23
"All Things Considered," 154
"All Winter in the Stern of a Lobster Boat," 57-58
Alice in Acidland, 141
Allums, Gail, 137-138
American, 2
American Collector, 3, 22
American Medical Association, 87
American Way, 119
American Weekly, 2
American Society of Journalists and Authors (ASJA), 40, 67, 77
Americana, 22
Animal Kingdom, 3
Antiquarian, The, 22
Antique Trader Weekly, The, 22
Antiques Journal, 22
"Apocalypse When? The Survivalists," 71-72
Argosy, 5, 23
Armadillos, 125-129
Arizona Highways, 123
Army Times, 83, 85
Art of Writing Non-fiction, The, 18, 76
Art News, 3
Articles and Features, 76
Asimov, Issac, 19
Atlantic Monthly, The, 58
Austin American-Statesman, The, 41
Austin magazine, 83-84

Baby Care, 3
Baker, Robert L., 107-115
Banks, Kelle, 83-84
Baptist Leader, The, 138
Beaver, 23
Becker, Stephen, 58-59
Bendiner, Bob, 18
Behrens, John C., 104-105
Bernstein, Theodore, 30
Best Magazine Articles: 1966, 70
Better Homes and Gardens, 61
Big Ten, 138

Bionic Woman, The, 19
Block, Jean Libman, 87
Black Spring, 39
Blakemore, Rick, 39, 55
Boone, Richard, 13
Bowen, Dr. Otis R., 87-88
Bowlers Journal & Billiard Review, 137-138, 140-141
Boyd, Alan S., 112-113
Boyle, Robert H., 53-54, 99
Bremner, John, 30
Bride's Magazine, 21
British Broadcasting System, 154
Brody, John, 83
Broussard, E. Joseph, 151
Bryant, Dr. Vaughn M. Jr., 130-137
Buchman, Dr. Dian Dincin, 77-78
"Building the Magazine Article," 24
Burroughs, William E., 38, 46
Bush, George, 65

Caidin, Martin, 19
Careful Writer, The, 30
Canadian Emergency Measures Organization, 13
Canadian Horse, The, 3
Cannery Row, 77
Cat Fancy, 3
Catholic Index, 28
Catholic Life, 138
Car and Driver, 3, 62-63
Cavalier, 6, 15, 23, 138-139, 141
CB radio, 18-19
Changing Magazine, The, 1, 30
Chic, 23
Churchill, Winston, 41
Chuckwagon, The, 62
Clark, Tim, 44
Cleveland, 3
Club, 23
Collectibles and Antiques Monthly, 22
Collector's News, 22
Collier's, 2
Complete Walker, The, 99
Conners, Robert J., 74
Copple, Neal, 94
Coprolites, 130-137
Coronet, 2

Cosell, Howard, 33, 36
Cosgrove, Benjamin Michael, 67
Cosgrove, Karen, 67
Cosmopolitan, 21, 80
Cott, Jonathan, 39
Cousins, Norman, 1
Cox, Mike, 41
Custom Van Magazine, 3
Cyborg, 19

D Magazine, 3
Daily Iowan, The, 137
Dallas Morning News, The, 71
Daniels, Judith, 77
Dapper, 23
Delta Books, 24
Dictionary of American Biography, 28
DiMaggio, Joe, 75-76
Discover, 143
DeVita, Dr. Vincent, 61
"Donahue Dossier, The," 56-57
Donahue, Phil, 56-57
Doss, Buster, 139-140
"Dumbarton Oaks: Stately link from past to the present," 51-52

Earl of Louisiana, The, 63
Early American Life, 22
Edel, Leon, 48-49
Elements of Style, The, 94
Elk's Magazine, The, 3, 117-121
Elliott, Osborn, 43
Emerson, Bill, 43
Endings:
  Add-on, 112
  Anecdotal, 112-113
  Echo, 114
  Lead Replay, 109-110
  Natural close, 113
  Proximity close, 110
  Play on words, 111-112
  Quote close, 112
  Restatement of purpose, 110-111
  Stinger, 114
  Straight statement close, 113-114
  Summary close, 113
  Word of advise close, 114
Escapade, 23
Esquire, 23, 75, 101, 117

Family Circle, 21, 120
Family Weekly, 40
Far West, 3
Farm Wife News, 21
Fawcett Books, 18
Ferragamo, Vince, 56
Few Minutes With Andy Rooney, A, 152
"Fighting History at 'Big White U,'" 65-66
Finding Facts: Interviewing, Observing, Using Reference Sources, 28
Fletcher, Colin, 99
Fling magazine, 23
Fontaine, Andre, 18, 50, 76
Franklin, Pete, 33-34
FreeLancer and Staff Writer, 79-80
Friedman, Thomas C., 70
Froeschle, Bob, 138

Gaines, William M., 1
Gallery, 23, 138
Gaillot, Una, 43-44
Gargan, Edward A., 97
Gehman, Richard, 1, 5, 50, 53
Gent, 23, 138
Gentleman's Quarterly, 23
Glamour, 21
Good Housekeeping, 21, 83, 87-88
Gnostica News, 121
Graham, Betsy, 29, 93-94
Grapes of Wrath, The, 24
Gregg Reference Manual, 30
Gourmet, 3
"Guide to Writing a *Popular Science* Article," 143-144
Guns of August, The, 48
Gunther, Max, 108

Halberstam, Dr. Michael, 96-98
Handbook of Nonsexist Writing, for Writers, Editors and Speakers, 94
Harper's Bazaar, 21
Hartley, William B., 24
"Has Anybody Here Seen Kelly?," 70
Hefner, Hugh, 1
Heinlein, Robert, 123
Hemingway, Ernest, 6, 15, 17, 75
Here at The New Yorker, 1
"Hey, Mister Fantasy Man," 69-70

Hibbs, Ben, 1
Higdon, Hal, 67-68, 77, 83, 85-89
Hill, David, 15
Hill, Diane, 15
Hill, Douglas, 15
Hill, Major, 9, 11
Hill, Norman, 9, 11
Hill, Wes, 5-16, 154-158
Hill, William, "Red," 9-10
Hill, William "Red Jr.," 10
Hilt, John, 86-87
Hirshberg, Lynn, 56
Holden, Larry, 116-122
Holgate, Jack F., 151
Holiday, 40
House Beautiful, 40, 73
Houston City magazine, 3
"How to Write and Sell an Article," 50
Hughes, Howard, 54-55
Hustler, 23

"In Praise of Southern Autumns," 68
Inc. magazine, 3
Indiana, University of, 87-88
Industrial Arts Index, 28
Information Please almanac, 30
Ingersoll, John, 73-74
Inside Story, 109
"Interview or The Only Wheel in Town, The," 35-36
International Yearbook and Statemen's Who's Who, 30
Iowa Alumni Review, 62, 138
Iowa, University of, 137

James, Henry, 48
Janssen, Richard E., 110
Jenner, Bruce, 69-70
Johnson, Lyndon Baines, 48
Journalistic Interview, The, 41
Joyce, James, 61

Kaercher, Dan, 61
Kaplan, Justin, 48
Kazin, Alfred, 48
Kearns, Doris, 48
"Kelly" (musical), 70
Kelly, George A., 35
Kelly, T.H., 59-60
Kenefick, John C., 112-113
King, Stephen, 51

Kilpatrick, James J., 68-69
Knight, 23

"L.A.'s Fight Song: We are Not Fam-i-lee," 56
Lady's Circle, 21
Ladies Home Journal, 21
Lampe, David, 40-41, 102, 123-137, 139
Laphan, Lewis, 70
Leads:
  Anecdotal, 55-56
  Classified Ad, 70-71
  Descriptive, 51-52
  Diary-Timeline, 65-66
  Dual narrative, 69
  False, 63-64
  First person, 57-59
  Flat statement, 61
  Future tense-fictional, 71-72
  Generalization, 76-77
  Humor, 76
  Interior monologue, 60-61
  Mosaic, 53-54
  Name prominent, 64-65
  Historical updating, 73-74
  Historical perspective, 74-75
  Narrative, 54-55
  Parody, 61-62
  Problem or paradox, 56-57
  Psychological, 75-76
  Question, 68-69
  Second person (you), 59-60
  Shotgun, 72-73
  Simile or metaphor, 62-63
  Summary, 51
  Unorthodox, 69-70
  What-where-when, 64
Lemon, Del, 33-34
Lennon, John, 96-98
Liberty, 2
Life, 2
Liebling, A.J., 1, 63
Lions and the Lambs, The, 140-141
Lindamood, Jean, 62-63
Los Angeles magazine, 80
Literary agents, 101-102
Literary Biography, 49
Look, 2
Long, Gov. Huey, 63
Luce, Henry, 1
Lussier, Jean, 9

Mad, 1
M.A.D.D., 25
Mademoiselle, 21
Magazine Article Writing, 29, 93-94
Magazine Writer's Workbook, The, 104-105
Magazines in the Twentieth Century, 1
Mailer, Norman, 92
Man Who Walked Through Time, The, 99
"Medical Breakthroughs that Could Lengthen Your Life," 61
Manchester Guardian, The, 40
Man to Man, 23
Marathon World, 130, 136-137
Marooned, 19
Matustik, Vicki, 73
McCalls, 21
McDermott, Barry, 56
McGivney, Annette, 62
McRoy, Dr. Ruth, 73
Metro, 121
Middle Man, The, 102
Mighty Niagara, The, 13
Mileti, Nick, 60
Miller, Casey, 94
Miller, Henry, 39
Modern Bride, 21
Modern English Usage, 30
Modern Feature Writing, 31
Modern People, 120-121
Money Making Tips, 121
"Monday Night Football," 36
Monroe, Marilyn, 75-76
Morgan, James, 117
Mother Earth News, 3
Morris, Greg, 61-62
"Mission: Impossible," 61-62
Mr., 23
"Mr. Mileti," 60
Ms., 21
Mutual Broadcasting Co., 85

NASA, 118
National Cancer Institute, 61
National Enquirer, The, 118-119
National Four-H News, 3
National Jewish Monthly, The, 138
National Public Radio, 157-158
National Wildlife magazine, 124-129
Nelson, Roy Paul, 50, 76-77
Nelson, Willie, 45, 139-140
New York magazine, 3, 77
New York Times, The, 96, 97
New Yorker, The, 1
New Republic Books, 48
Newspaper "Help" Columns, 30
Newspaper morgues, 29-30
Newsweek, 43, 70, 103
Nike Sport Research Labs., 68
"Non-fiction: Postal Mortem," 83
Non-sexist writing style, 94
Nugget magazine, 23, 138

"Ode to the age of the Beetle," 74
Olmert, Michael, 51
Ottum, Bob, 69
Oui magazine, 23, 85, 120, 138
Oman, Fred, 121
Omni, 143
Outline, Writing the, 23-24, 31
"On Being a Patient," 58-59
On Reporting the News, 38, 46
On Writing Well, 92-93

PLO, 70-71
Pachter, Marc, 48-49
Parachutist magazine, 3
Parade, 40, 130, 136
People, 83, 86-87
Penthouse, 23, 138
Perlmutter, Jerome, 24-25
"Pete Franklin Show, The," 33-34
Peterson, Theodore, 1
Philadelphia, 3
"Pig of Bronze," 62-63
Playboy, 1, 23, 51, 85, 138
Playgirl, 21, 120-121
Popular Mechanics, 40
Popular Science, 27, 31, 40, 46-48, 143-149
Poyner, Jim, 71-72
Practical Guide to Effective Writing, A, 24-25
Private Pilot, 3
Publication rights, 138-139
Pulitzer Prize, 48
Purdy, Ken, 1, 47

Query Letters, 23, 79-83
    Examples of, 84-89
Quotation Marks, use of, 94-95

Ratcliffe, Jack, 18
Reader's Digest, 1, 80
Reader's Guide to Periodical Literature, 21-22, 23, 26, 28
Reagan, Ronald, 65
Redbook, 21
Reddick, DeWitt, 31
Redford, Robert, 74
"Reflections of a Cosmic Tourist: An Afternoon With Henry Miller," 39
Relics, 22
Reporter, The, 40
Reynolds, Paul R., 102
Richardson, Elliot, 44-45
Rivers, William, L., 28, 50, 79-80
Rock & Gem, 3
Roget II, 30
Rolling Stone, 39, 56
Rollins, Jeanne, 57-58
Rooney, Andy, 152
Rosen, R.D., 56
Rosengarten, Theodore, 48
Ross, Harold, 1
Ruehlman, William, 17-18, 151
Rummel, Archbishop John, 43-44
Runner, The, 67-68
"Running Through Pregnancy," 67

Salancik, Jerry, 35
Saturday Review of Literature, 1, 40
Saturday Evening Post, The, 1, 2, 70, 85
Savvy, 77
Scene magazine, 73
Schneler, Donald, 99
Scheck, Ken, 103
Science Digest, 130-136, 143
Screw, 23
"Sentinel at Niagara Falls," 5-16, 56, 154-158
Sepia, 138
Seven Days in May, 71
Seventeen, 117
"Shadows on the Wall," 68
"She Plumb Give It All Away," 53
Sherwood, Hugh C., 41
Signature, 124
"Silent Season of a Hero, The," 75-76
Sir, 23
Six Million Dollar Man, The, 19

"Sixty Minutes," 85
Skipol, Art, 83
Skydiving, 19
Smithsonian, 40, 51, 99
Smokeys, Truckers, CB Radios & You, 18
Smolkin, Shelly, 50, 79-80
"So You Want to be a Free-Lance Writer?," 103
Society of Author's Representatives (SAR), 102
Southwest Arts, 3
Spielberg, Steven, 56
Sports Illustrated, 53, 56, 59-60, 69, 124
Stalking the Feature Story, 17
Stamberg, Susan, 154
Statistics in non-fiction, 96-98
Startling Detective, 3
Stathakis, George, 9
Steinbeck, John, 24, 77
Stephens, Charles, 9
Stilwell and the American Experience in China, 48
Stolley, Richard, 86
Storm, Tempest, 46
Story: The Yearbook of Discovery, 1969, 141
"Strange Fish and Stranger Times of Dr. Herbert R. Axelrod, The," 53-54
Streisand, Barbara, 74
Strunk, William, 94
Sunset, 3
Susskind, Hal, 84
Swank, 23, 138
Sweatt, Heman Marion, 65-66
Swift, Kate, 94
Synonym Finder, The, 30

TWA Ambassador, 117
Talese, Gay, 75-76
Talk, 120
Tape recorders, 37-38, 147
Taylor, Anne, 8
Teece, David, 65-66
Telling Lives: The Biographer's Art, 48
Terkel, Studs, 85
Texas A & M University, 130-137
Texas Girl, 139

Texas Highways, 123-124
Texas Monthly, 3
Texas Restaurant Association, 62
Texas, University of (Austin), 65-66, 73
Theft of ideas, 103
Thompson, Hunter, 92
Thousand-Mile Summer, The, 99
Time, Inc., 1
This Week, 2
Thurber, James, 1
Titles, 104-105
Transitions, 98-100
Travolta, John, 101
Trikilis, Ted, 117, 120
True, 5, 40
Trippett, Frank, 43
Tuchman, Barbara W., 48
"Turn Your Home Into a Solar Collector," 73-74
"Turning Magazine Articles into Books," 140-141
Twain, Mark, 48

UPI, 85, 87
UPI Stylebook, 94-95
Understanding Magazines, 30
University Microfilms, 29
"Urban Cowboy," 101

Viva, 21
Vogue, 21

WFAA, 85
WWWE, 33
Wall Street Journal, The, 110
Wallace, DeWitt, 1
Wallace, Lila, 1
Washington Journalism Review, 56
Watt, James, 70
Way We Were, The, 74
Wayward Reporter: The Life of A.J. Liebling, 1
Webb, Eugene J., 35
Webster's Biographical Dictionary, 30
Webster's Geographical Dictionary, 30
Webster's New World Dictionary, 30
Weight Watchers, 3
"Where Nothing But Good Happens," 59-60

Whitaker 81 (almanac), 30
Whitman, Walt, 48
Wicker, Tom, 96-98
Wildlife, 124
Wiley, Gale, 83, 85, 150-158
"Will Hollywood's Mr. Perfect Ever Grow Up?," 56
Wolfe, Tom, 92
Wolff, Geoffrey, 48
Wolseley, Roland E., 1, 30
Woman's Day, 21
Woman's Home Companion, 2
Women's Circle, 22
Words on Words, 30
Working, 85
World of Oz, The, 43-44
Writer, The, 24
Writer's Digest, 83, 116, 122, 140-141
Writer's Market, 3, 21-23, 26, 82-83
Writing and Reporting Broadcast News, 151
White, E.B., 94

Yankee, 3, 44-45, 57-58, 74

Zinsser, William, 33, 92-94
Zimroth, Peter L., 97
Zolotow, Maurice, 80
Zucker, Dr. Louis, 73

About the author...

Thomas Fensch has been a magazine freelancer since 1967. His articles have appeared in a wide variety of publications including many of the men's magazines; his reviews have appeared in the book pages of *The Chicago Sun-Times* and other major newspapers. He is the author of six previous books of non-fiction, published since 1970, which have been successful, commercially and critically. His *Smokeys, Truckers, CB Radios & You* sold 74,800 copies in two years and his *Steinbeck and Covici: The Story of a Friendship* won the Martha Kinney Cooper Ohioana Book of the Year in Biography award in late 1980. He is a member of the American Society of Journalists and Authors and is on the faculty of the College of Communication, The University of Texas at Austin.

He holds his B.A. degree from Ashland (Ohio) College, his M.A. from The University of Iowa, and his Ph.D. in Communications from Syracuse University. Dr. Fensch is an exception to the old rule: *those who can, do; those who can't, teach.*